What Color is the Other Side of Darkness?

Lessons of Living Taught by the Dying

By Jean Roche, RSM

Fort Orange Press, Inc.

ISBN: 1-933994-05-3
ISBN-13: 978-1-933994-5-5

CREDITS:

Cover photo taken by author, Jean Roche, at The Cenacle, Lantana, Florida

Meaghan Leary art work on this page and pages 1, 16, 20, 35, 41, 48, 56, 62, 103, 122, 133
Joe Faul art work on page 35

Barbara Roman, RSM, art work on page 127

Introduction

W hen I was but a "baby" hospice chaplain, a patient asked, "What color is the other side of darkness?" Overwhelmed by the nature of the question, I stammered in return, "Gee Molly, I don't know. What color do you think it is?" Being Irish, she responded that it simply had to be green.

Often since then I have pondered that profound question, and it occurs to me, that whenever darkness comes into our lives, whatever its shape or form, the natural human inclination is to flee: to run away from it, jump over it, crawl under it, seek any way of circumventing it. Yet the thousands of hospice patients whom I have accompanied have taught me that it is only in going through it that we come to the other side which is undeniably light.

As the Bible says, "the gift you have received, give as a gift," so is this book a humble effort to share the inspiration, courage, grace and transformational power evoked by those to whom I have ministered for nearly two decades.

While long ago I had been given verbal permission to share these stories, in the interest of confidentiality, names, specific details, and inconsequential circumstances have been altered. In some cases, two stories have been interwoven. Universal themes, however, have been preserved. It is my hope that the reader will become aware of the sacredness of each story and its connection to the Greater Story of our common humanity.

Acknowledgements

I give thanks, first and foremost, to each hospice patient and family whom I was privileged to serve. They have, quite literally, transformed my own life, grounding me in gratitude for the gift of the present moment and reminding me that it is never too late to reconcile relationships and celebrate life.

I am grateful also to the following persons: Maria College students who encouraged me to share these stories more broadly, especially Chuck Carhart and Jen Griswold; to Agnes Stillman who typed the first draft; and Vivian Cripps who continued the project; to the astute and insightful Julia Mary Werner, RSM, who critiqued this work; to the hospice staff, a veritable spiritual community with whom I shared this mission of mercy; to Bill Wilson whose original hospice logo graces the title page of this book; to Eleanor Guerin, RSM, and Agnes Stillman who were tenacious in pursuing copyright permissions and to artists Meaghan Leary, Joe Faul, and Barbara Roman, RSM, whose talents have so enhanced these stories; to Chloe Van Aken for her assistance with layout and a myriad of other unforeseen tasks and lastly to the Sisters of Mercy who have always affirmed my gifts and offered their spiritual and practical support.

Dedication

This book is dedicated to God,
the Ultimate Author
of these sacred stories.

How to Use this Book

1. Find a quiet time and place where you can read a story undisturbed.

2. Erase from the blackboard of your mind all distractions and concerns in order to give your full attention to each story.

3. Read slowly and reverently.

4. You may wish to enter into the story with your imagination, utilizing senses of sight, sound, taste and touch, and visualizing yourself as one of the participants in the vignette.

5. Spend some time reflecting on how the story connects with your own.

6. Contemplate the spiritual exercise suggested at the end of each story — or devise one of your own.

7. Use the space provided to sketch or make notes on what the story evoked in you.

8. Another suggestion is to purchase a journal or art journal to record your reflections and insights in greater detail — or to begin the writing of your own story.

Contents

What's in a Name?

Rocco, nicknamed Rocky after his dad's idol, Rocky Marciano, was a forty-five year old macho ex-marine who came to our hospice in-patient facility to die. His body was covered with tattoos of ferocious beasts and snakes, a metaphorical message to "keep out." He growled at staff members, saying, "I know I'm going to die, but I don't want to talk about it, so bug off!"

Since my last name is "Roche," I offered a lighthearted pun on the appropriateness of having been told to "bug off," whereupon Rocky burst into laughter. That moment of light-heartedness enabled me to get my little toe in the door of his heart. Subsequently, he shared the story of his life, one of having "sown wild oats" across the country and beyond. "I've not been close to God," he concluded, "and I probably should do something about it now, but I feel like a hypocrite because the truth is I'm only doing it because I'm going to die."

Reminded of the biblical story of the Prodigal Son, an account of a wild and recalcitrant young man who was gratu-itously welcomed home by a loving father, Rocky expressed hope that God would view him with similar compassion. In fact, to my surprise, he concluded our first meeting by offering this prayer:

O God, I'm sorry I've left you out of my life all these years.
And I hope you will forgive me.
And if you don't, the hell with you!

1

Not a bad beginning, I reflected. Subsequently, the song "I Am a Rock" surfaced in my consciousness and I brought it in to play for Rocky. Tears streamed down his face as he listened and acknowledged that he was not a rock at all, but a vulnerable human being filled with fear. Having listened at length to his trepidations, and noticing also his low esteem due to disparaging names given to him by his father, I later paraphrased an excerpt from the Book of Isaiah in which God says:

I have loved you with an everlasting love . . .
There is nothing you could have done or failed to do
That can separate you from my love . . .
And I want to give you a new name:
It is Loved-by-God.

We had his new name calligraphied and hung at his bedside.

Having experienced a sense of reconciliation with his Creator, Rocky decided that, like the Prodigal Son, he, too, wanted to have a party to celebrate. Encouraged to do so, he invited seventy-five friends, including his barroom buddies, and arranged to be "roasted" by a voluptuous woman dressed up like a bunny. During this process, it became evident that just as Rocky had himself been given negative nicknames, so had he passed on epithets of deprecation to others. His wife was called "Stupid"; his daughter, "Lard-Ass" or "Pork-Ass"; a best friend, "Fish-Lips"; and a well-endowed relative, "Tits."

After the party, Rocky's condition began to decline rapidly and he expressed the desire to leave his family a meaningful legacy. "It can't be money because I don't have any," he muttered, "and I don't want to make a video because then they could turn me off!"

I suggested that, just as he had received a new name, perhaps the best gift he could bestow upon his family would be to rename them. The initial response was, at best, a grudging one, but he indicated that he would give the idea some thought.

Shortly before he died, Rocky summoned me to his room where his wife sat on one side of the bed, his daughter on the other. "Sister Jean," he said proudly, "I want you to know I've given my wife and daughter new names."

Turning to his spouse, he said, "You're not 'Stupid' anymore." My new name for you is 'My Honey.' He proceeded to thank her for her love and faithfulness and asked forgiveness for the times he was M.I.A. — missing-in-action — from their marriage.

He then addressed his lovely eight-year-old daughter, saying, "You're not "Lard-Ass" or "Pork-Ass" anymore. Daddy's new name for you is 'Little Star.'" The child's smile lit up the room in what was clearly a transformational moment.

It is said that the concrete image is symbolic of the spiritual fact. Thus, as a parting gift, I presented Rocky and his family with a geode, a rock which is non-descript on the outside, but when split open, reveals amethyst crystals. I told them that because Rocky had allowed himself to be penetrated by love, we were able to discover his inner beauty, goodness and grace. At his wake service, his daughter placed half of the geode in his coffin, keeping the other half as a reminder of her trust in their ultimate reconnection.

The culminating gift of the experience for me came months later in the form of a reminder that my own name "Roche" means "rock" in French. The walls of a stoic Irish defense system came down as I read a mystical poem reminding me that flowers do not spring forth from stone. I resolved to become earth instead, that I might manifest flowers of myriad colors.

Spiritual Exercise

List the names you have been called throughout your life, including nicknames, roles and titles. Note the feelings evoked by each one. Spend some time reflecting on your essence or unique gift, allowing a new name to surface in your consciousness.

You may wish to invite others to participate in the process or plan a simple ritual to honor this deeper manifestation of your Higher Self. Another option is to create an artistic calligraphy featuring your new name.

_____

_____

_____

_____

_____

_____

_____

_____

_____

_____

_____

_____

_____

Create an artistic representation of your new name below.

Letting Go

Beatrice had been extremely close to her spouse, Bill. Both were recovering alcoholics and their relationship was described by some as "enmeshed" or "co-dependent." Nevertheless, their mutual love had been palpable and expressed in myriad ways.

When Bill died of cirrhosis of the liver, Bea was devastated. She carried the urn containing his ashes everywhere she went. They rested on the seat of his lounge chair or at the kitchen table where he often sat. She carried on daily conversations as if he were actually physically present.

This went on for many months. After countless sessions with a bereavement counselor, Bea decided she was ready to scatter Bill's ashes at a woodland location where they often picnicked, sharing apples. A ceremony was planned.

With great difficulty and paroxysms of sobbing, Bea let go of Bill's remains, scattering them to the wind. Later, a few friends sat with her on a log in the woods eating apples in remembrance of the couple's favorite ritual. They sat in silence watching the autumn leaves slowly drift to earth.

After expressing relief at finally having had the courage to let go of Bill's ashes, Bea began to share her awareness of the many other things she needed to relinquish if she was to be free to move on. It appeared that as each leaf fell, she named it and sought to let go: e.g. anger that Bill had died and left her alone; rage at physicians who had promised to cure him;

guilt at the times she had lost patience while caring for him; fear that she would not be able to make it on her own. When she had finished, each of her friends shared something they needed to let go of as well in order to continue the journey to greater freedom and peace.

This spontaneous part of the ritual was concluded by a verbatim recitation of the following poem:

Autumn Sonnet
by May Sarton
If I can let you go as trees let go
Their leaves, so casually, one by one;
If I can come to know what they do know,
That fall is the release, the consummation,
Then fear of time and the uncertain fruit
Would not distemper the great lucid skies
This strangest autumn, mellow and acute
If I can take the dark with open eyes
And call it seasonal, nor harsh or strange
(For love itself may need a time of sleep),
And, treelike, stand unmoved before the change,
Lose what I lose to keep what I can keep,
The strong root still alive under the snow,
Love will endure — if I can let you go.

Spiritual Exercise
There is a Native American tradition of writing down burdensome thoughts, negative messages or troublesome concerns. These writings then are placed in a decorated basket which is representative of the Divine embrace. Plan and implement such a ritual for yourself or a group. Another option is simply to make a list of what you need to relinquish

in order to continue your journey to greater freedom and
peace.

In order to continue my journey to greater freedom and
peace, I need to let go of:

_____

_____

_____

_____

_____

_____

_____

_____

_____

_____

_____

_____

_____

Facing Death

William was a ten-year-old child with leukemia. He came to the hospice in-patient unit for terminal care. Although both ambulatory and lucid, he was expected to die within weeks, possibly due to an internal bleed. His parents were attentive, taking turns being with him so that he would never be alone. Occasionally, he went out for rides with his dad or baked cookies with his hospice nurses. He became an assistant to the hospice chaplain, helping to set up for weekly prayer services or sharing a personal prayer.

William had a twelve-year-old sister Joanie. Her needs had been eclipsed by the attention showered upon her brother. Thus she became withdrawn and morose; her grades in school also suffered. Apparently, there were no adult confidantes and Joanie was reticent to talk with her peers about what was happening. Furthermore, she had been avoiding visiting her brother, fearful that he might die while she was there. Her parents sought to maintain a semblance of normalcy at home so there had been virtually no familial discussion. Thus a hospice volunteer was assigned to offer support and comfort to Joanie.

William, an affable, outgoing child, often visited other patients, evoking their stories and feelings in a disarming manner. Highly imaginative, William envisioned his chemotherapy as white warriors coming to his defense. A recent drawing, however, had revealed William's awareness that the white warriors had themselves been slain by a dark, ominous foe.

Yet, William, with childlike simplicity and faith, remained unafraid. Often visited by a contemplative priest, he found solace in prayer. Shortly before his death, William held his own family meeting, thanking his family and professional caregivers for helping him. Expressing his joyful expectancy of meeting his deceased grandmother in heaven, he told Joanie not to be afraid. Family members had an opportunity to bless William, expressing their love and gratitude. William reciprocated, offering each one a loving and thankful message. Shortly after this moving family meeting, William died peacefully.

Spiritual Exercise

Recall an experience in your familial or professional life when you, like Joanie, felt eclipsed by the needs or the light of another person. What was that like for you? Or, perhaps you have neglected yourself, be it your own body, mind, soul or spirit. Write a letter of affirmation to your "neglected self."

_____

_____

_____

_____

_____

_____

_____

_____

_____

_____

_____

_____

_____

_____

_____

_____

_____

_____

_____

_____

_____

_____

_____

Marvin the Miser

I f ever anyone was a contemporary embodiment of
Ebenezer Scrooge, it was Marvin, a hospice home care
patient who even looked the part of the notorious protag-
onist of *A Christmas Carol*. Rimless glasses perched on the end
of his nose, he glowered at me with beady little eyes on my
first visit — and then commanded Mary, his sister and primary care giver, to read the definition of the word "miser."
Mary read: "An extremely covetous person who for the sake
of wealth makes himself miserable."

"That's me," scowled Marvin. "I've been a miser all my life,
and all I've cared about is making money." He explained that
his business had been his primary concern, leaving little time
for personal relationships. Mary had taken her brother to live
with her after learning of his terminal illness. Undaunted by
Marvin's harsh façade, I continued to visit him regularly and
grew to like him.

One day, to my surprise, Marvin said he was planning a
reconciliation with his nephew, Lawrence, from whom he had
been estranged for some time. He explained that although he
was going to die soon, Lawrence was still a young man who
would have to carry the burden of their unresolved conflict
for the rest of his life. Since Lawrence was already on his way
to see Marvin, traveling hundreds of miles, I commented that
he must care about his uncle very much.

His newfound burst of compassion suddenly dissipating,

Marvin snarled, "You know why he's coming, don't you? He's after my money!"

Later, I anxiously inquired about the reunion. With tears trickling down his wrinkled cheeks, Marvin told me: "Lawrence called me uncle for the first time, and he told me he had always loved me but I had pushed him away. He hugged me and we both cried. And do you know what?" he concluded triumphantly, "He never once asked about my money!"

Marvin continued to blossom as slowly and beautifully as a flower in spring. This gradual transformation was further revealed after an altercation with Mary because she had spent some time on the porch with her friends. "At first I was angry," he said. "After all, here I am in here dying and she's out there talking and laughing with her friends." On further reflection, however, he realized that his sister had sacrificed a lot for him and needed some diversion as well as support and camaraderie.

Then Marvin shared with me a two-page prayer he had written to God, asking for forgiveness for his miserly ways and self-centered life. He thanked God for Mary and for the members of the hospice staff — who, he was reasonably sure, were not after his money.

Shortly before he died, Marvin told me he had awakened at 2 AM terrified because he knew he was going to die soon. He remembered hearing Mary talk about entrusting herself to God. "At the time, I really didn't know what she meant," he said, "but last night I was so afraid, I did it. I entrusted myself to God, and I was filled with the greatest sense of peace and joy I have ever known."

Marvin died shortly thereafter, but not before I shared with him and Mary a reflection I had written about the miracle of Marvin's transformation:

To Marvin with Love

Like a magnificent butterfly
you emerged from the cocoon
of a parsimonious nature,
leaving behind as inconsequential the casement
which kept you in and others out.
Your wings were weak at first,
dampened by your tears,
until soft winds of love dried them,
freeing you to sail aloft
to a trysting place
with your God — and us.

Spiritual Exercise

Write a letter of reconciliation to someone from whom you feel estranged or design a ritual to help you befriend a part of yourself which you have sought to disown.

_____

_____

_____

_____

_____

_____

_____

_____

_____

_____

_____

_____

_____

_____

_____

_____

_____

_____

_____

_____

_____

_____

_____

_____

_____

_____

Light in the Darkness

S amuel was an eighty-year-old man with liver cancer. Although Jewish in terms of religious rootedness, he was not connected to any synagogue and was vociferous in his expression of doubt about the existence of God, challenging caregivers to "prove it." His caustic wit was a thin veneer for his history of childhood abuse and abandonment. His father allegedly had deserted the family when Samuel was only five years old. His mother felt unable to care for him, so he was "bounced like a ball" from foster home to foster home. Samuel reported that his mother often told him how ugly he was, resulting in his avoidance of mirrors until he was into his twenties, lest his reflection prove his mother's judgment true.

Samuel shared graphic stories of having been beaten by foster parents upon minimal provocation. Once, on Christmas Eve, for example, he had crept into the living room to place two ornaments, which he had made, on the tree. Upon having been discovered by his foster father, he was struck with a strap for seeking to spy on Santa Claus.

Just when Samuel had found a happy home with a compassionate couple, his mother had remarried and "took him back" when he was fourteen. He had an abrasive relationship with his stepfather who took the boy out of school insisting that he get a job as a manual laborer.

Self-educated, Samuel eventually accepted a position with

a book company and married a devoted woman, Stella. She had died many years earlier. In the midst of the recounting of the dark side of his life, Samuel brightened as he spoke of his gift for writing poetry. "Would you like to hear one?" he asked and without waiting for an answer, began to recite:

To My Wife on the Toilet

O beautiful queen
Sitting on your throne,
Why are you sitting there
All alone?

As queen consort
Should I not be
Sitting in honor
Next to thee?

And she presumably
Answered:
This throne,
My darling,
Has but one seat
And it would be
A miraculous feat,
A feat, my darling,
To astonish the masses:
A single throne
For a couple of asses!

Tears flowed down Samuel's cheeks as he roared with laughter and glee at his own cleverness. As time went on, Samuel became more open and shared some of his more meaningful poetry. During one healing ritual, a song for the wounded child was played:

How could anyone ever tell you
You were anything less than beautiful?

> *How could anyone ever tell you*
> *You were less than whole?*
> *How could anyone fail to notice*
> *That your loving is a miracle?*
> *How deeply you're connected to my soul.*

This mantra, repeated over and over, had a profound effect on Samuel. A staff member, seeking to express Samuel's transfiguration tangibly, drew a mandala and placed it at his bedside. It had a black background with a wide yellow streak of lightning and these words:

> *Like a streak of lightning*
> *On a dark summer sky,*
> *Samuel's humor illuminated*
> *A shadowy landscape*
> *Of childhood abuse and*
> *Abandonment,*
> *Bathing the scene*
> *In redemptive light.*
>
> *Deo Gracias*

Shortly before Samuel's death, he became more restless and had been restrained in a lounge chair. "Goddam it, untie me!" he shouted, curling up into a fetal position. Gently massaging his hands, a caregiver untied him and prayed, "Samuel, I pray that you will be released from the bonds of bitterness and hurt which have held you captive for a lifetime." Samuel died peacefully in his room shortly thereafter, in the midst of a thunderstorm with bolts of lightning illuminating his room.

Spiritual Exercise

List the light and shadow experiences of your childhood, including a lesson learned from each one.

Unmasking

Dennis was a bright, charming young artist who was afflicted with the disease of AIDS. Well-versed in literature, he enjoyed acting and was also a model featured in well-known magazines. His home was filled with his lovely paintings of mountains, flowers and bubbling streams.

When asked about his personal life, Dennis responded by reciting verbatim the poem *Richard Cory:*

> *Whenever Richard Cory went downtown,*
> *We people on the pavement looked at him:*
> *He was a gentleman from sole to crown,*
> *Clean favored, and imperially slim.*
>
> *And he was always quietly arrayed,*
> *And he was always human when he talked;*
> *But still he fluttered pulses when he said,*
> *"Good morning," and he glittered when he walked.*
>
> *And he was rich—yes, richer than a king*
> *And admirably schooled in every grace:*
> *In fine, we thought he was everything*
> *To make us wish that we were in his place.*
>
> *So on we worked, and waited for the light,*
> *And went without meat, and cursed the bread;*
>
> *And Richard Cory, one calm summer night*
> *Went home and put a bullet through his head.*

> —Edward Arlington Robinson, *Richard Cory*

That the poem epitomized the young man's life was clear, for beneath a suave exterior, cloaked with the success of a lucrative theatrical career, lay a heart of quiet desperation. Accentuated by the diagnosis of AIDS, issues of identity became paramount. As Dennis was stripped of his masks and roles, he angrily stated, "I used to be known by names like Artist, Friend, or Actor; now, I'm nothing more than AIDS Victim!"

His spiritual caregiver pointed out that his disease was divesting him of his illusions, and she shared with him another poem:

> We wear the mask that grins and lies,
> it hides our cheeks and shades our eyes,
> This debt we pay to human guile,
> with torn and bleeding hearts we smile;
> and mouth with myriad subtleties. . . .
> Why should the world be overwise
> in counting all our tears and sighs,
> No, let them only see us while we wear the mask...
>
> We wear the mask,
> but O great Christ,
> Our cries to thee from tortured souls
> arise,
> but let them only see us
> while we wear the mask.

—Paul Lawrence Dunbar, *We Wear the Mask*

With tears washing away his mask, Dennis was finally able to share the cries of his tortured soul, which proved to be a powerful preamble to his spiritual healing. Elaborating, he described an abrasive relationship with his mother who had died of a heart attack during an argument with him. As a result, he lived with the burden of guilt and the conviction that he had been responsible for his mother's death. Though aware of his homosexuality, Dennis had suppressed it and married a young woman to please his Irish Catholic family. When the marriage failed, he became involved with a bevy of male lovers, acknowledging that his promiscuity was a flight from intimacy. His guilt was accentuated by the awareness that he had most likely passed on the disease of AIDS to others. Grief over the loss of friends and lovers also weighed heavily on Dennis' heart.

Encouraged to create a painting depicting the suffering of his life, Dennis shared with his spiritual caregiver a self-portrait which was also a Christ portrait. Asked to talk about this work of art, Dennis began to compare his suffering to that of Christ. He said that while the wounds of Christ were unjustly inflicted, his cancerous lesions were manifestations of his innate evil. Having been told by a priest that his homosexuality was unacceptable, Dennis was convinced that his disease was a manifestation of God's negative judgment.

The spiritual caregiver shared with him the account of Jesus' intervention in the stoning of the adulterous woman (John 8:1-10) and suggested instead that his wounds might symbolize a virtual self-inflicted stoning by his incessant harsh condemnation of his own actions and activities. A subsequent forgiveness ritual assisted Dennis in letting go of his self-hatred as he literally and figuratively "dropped the stone."

In time, he had a touching reconciliation with his former wife, each forgiving the other for hurts inflicted. Shortly before his death, Dennis had an art show displaying his finest works born of both the light and shadow of his life.

Spiritual Exercise

Use this space to draw a picture of the masks you have worn.

Write a prayer from the heart of your "Unmasked Self."

_____

_____

_____

_____

_____

_____

_____

_____

_____

_____

_____

_____

_____

_____

_____

_____

Peeling the Onion

Colleen was an attractive, dynamic elementary school teacher admitted to the hospice home care program subsequent to her diagnosis of metastatic breast cancer. A single woman, she was tended by her mother and several young teachers with whom she had worked.

As her death neared, Colleen began to reflect on her life and its meaning. Ira Progoff journaling exercises helped her to revisit the stepping stones of her life, including the "roads not taken."

One of the major crossroads in her life had been a broken wedding engagement. Eyes brimming with tears, she recounted the story of her previous intention to marry a handsome athlete whom she had met in high school. The wedding date had been set; her wedding dress purchased. Several wedding showers yielded gifts of silver and china. She had even submitted her resignation to the principal of the school in which she taught first grade.

As the date neared, however, Colleen felt overwhelmed by a lack of peace and precipitously broke the engagement. She and her fiancé parted with minimal communication. Paths having diverged, they soon lost touch with one another.

As she lay dying, however, Colleen acknowledged that she had never forgotten Matthew. She regretted the pain she had inflicted upon him and wondered if he had ever found happiness. Searching her soul, furthermore, she anguished regarding the possibility that she had made the wrong decision. Perhaps she had suffered only from the last minute trepidation known as "cold feet" and had foolishly, forever relinquished her dream of being a wife and mother.

One night, Colleen had a dream in which she and Matthew were holding a huge onion. It was purple and white. On awakening, she said that the dream had heightened her awareness that she had never grieved the losses inherent in her broken engagement. She viewed the colors as especially significant, purple being symbolic of healing and harmony, and white being an omen of peace.

Meanwhile, Matthew, who lived in a nearby city had learned of Colleen's imminent demise. He, too, was plagued by memories of the past and the unfinished business which had resulted from their separation. Friends of both Colleen and Matthew, having discerned a mutual receptivity, arranged a meeting between the two.

The reunion was both tender and emotional. Each acknowledged perduring love for the other. They laughed over their follies – and cried as sheaves of the metaphorical onion were peeled away.

Reflecting on the past, Colleen confessed her fear that Matthew would one day cease to love her. He, in turn, admitted to doubt that he could ever have fulfilled her expectations. He also acknowledged a deep-seated feeling that he was unworthy of her love. Each sought to reassure the other. Their meeting concluded with a mutual exchange of heartfelt blessings.

Colleen felt at peace after the meeting with Matthew, though she remained wistful that she had never been a mother. Seeking to cheer her, friends created a huge report card for Colleen, bestowing exemplary grades in areas such as devotion to duty, faithful friendship and the mothering of hundreds of first graders entrusted to her care.

When Colleen died, her primary care physician, appreciative of the spiritual care her patient had received, donated a large sum of money to the hospice. It was used to create ten spiritual care kits for hospice home care nurses. Within each substantial tote bag was an exquisite stained glass candle holder purchased from a local artist as well as resources of music, candles, creative rituals, meditations and prayer. In keeping with Colleen's mission of education, these were presented at a workshop on "Tools of Psycho-Spiritual Care".

Spiritual Exercise

As the mystic Rumi says: "Don't' turn your head / Dare to look at the bandaged place / That's where the light enters," so you are invited to reflect on the losses of your life using the Major Loss Inventory in the Appendix as a springboard to further healing.

Legacy of Love

J oe was a fifty-two-year-old seemingly robust Irishman. His good looks belied the hidden cancer slowly but inexorably eating away his life. Realistic about his prognosis, he nevertheless remained optimistic, focusing on meaningful relationships with his wife and three children. As he declined, he contemplated how he might say goodbye and leave this life gracefully, bestowing his legacy of love in a farewell ritual to include a blessing of his loved ones.

Integral to the planned ceremony had been the family coat of arms which Joe deeply revered. On a recent trip to Ireland, however, Joe had discovered that some of his ancestors on the Emerald Isle had been bandits and among the things they reportedly had stolen was the coat of arms. Their name was Reedy, but they had taken the Ruddy coat of arms! Crestfallen, Joe confided in me his disappointment. I responded, "Why not create your own coat of arms?"

Eyes widening with wonder and delight, Joe responded with alacrity, enthusiastically planning a familial work of art. Spanning the coat of arms was to be a rainbow, symbolic of Joe's view of the all-pervasive presence of God, as well as his wife's colorful personality and enduring love. He chose the figure of a pregnant woman to represent one daughter who, he said, "has always been a life-bearer in this family." Another symbol was that of a woman playing a harp to reflect the musical gifts of another daughter whose melodies invariably lifted his heart and spirit. His son was portrayed in a pictorial vignette, including a heart and anchor to signify his having been rooted in love since his marriage.

For himself, Joe selected a sketch of a contemporary Good Samaritan, for he had often reached out to the needy, particularly drug addicted teens. The Irish and American flags, a Celtic cross and Marine insignia were among the salient additions planned for the coat of arms. A local artist was commissioned to carry out Joe's instructions.

Sadly, Joe died, somewhat precipitously, before the work was completed, but it was presented to the family as a surprise at the memorial service, a veritable gift from the grave.

Spiritual Exercise

Create your own coat of arms, or write a letter of affirmation to your loved ones articulating the "legacy" you wish to leave them. Include cherished values, hopes, dreams and lessons born of both the light and shadow of your life.

Use this space to create your own coat of arms.

Write a letter of affirmation to your loved ones here.

Ain't Never Gonna Go

Consuela was a sixty-five-year-old Sister of Mercy who was so fearful of facing death that she had discharged herself from the hospice program and returned to the convent where she had been living since her illness.

Continuing to visit as a friend rather than in my official capacity as a hospice chaplain, I encouraged her to share what had been meaningful in her life. Brightening visibly, she exclaimed, "I won a prize for a children's story I wrote in college. The name of it was *Ain't Never Gonna Go.*" Gulping at what appeared to be an obvious analogy, I encouraged her to tell me more.

She explained that it was a story about a child who was fearful of the principal of the school, having heard so many scary stories about her. One day, after the students had been asked to draw pictures of a summer vacation, the child was told to take his picture to show to the principal. "With feet like bricks, he walked down the long, dark scary corridor to the principal's office and, with tremulous hand and pounding heart, he knocked on the door." Slowly, it swung open to reveal a smiling lady who welcomed him warmly and gazed in admiration at his drawing. "'Why, I can almost feel the warmth of the sun and hear the seagulls,'" she said while offering him candy as a reward.

Having been encouraged to use the story as a visualization, entering into it imaginatively using all of her senses, Consuela came to a sense of identification with the child in the story and concluded that at the end of the long dark scary corridor which was her death, there awaited her a smiling lady, Our Lady of Mercy, longing to say to her, "Consuela, what a wonderful painting you've created with your life."

Spiritual Exercise

Choose a fairy tale, biblical story or myth with which you identify in some special way. Dialogue with one of the key characters or draw a picture placing yourself in a salient scene from the story.

Use this space for your drawing.

Write your dialogue with a key character in a fairy tale, biblical story or myth here.

_____

_____

_____

_____

_____

_____

_____

_____

_____

_____

_____

_____

_____

_____

_____

The Viking Spirit

Hagar was a fifty-eight-year-old man with chronic obstructive pulmonary disease. He lived with his wife, Helga. Both were originally from Norway and had one son who lived at a distance.

A macho man, Hagar loved to reminisce about the rigors of his life as a fisherman in Norway and later, working on the docks of New York City. He was proud of his heritage and, when well, enjoyed the company, food, drink and dance of fellow Norwegians who had come to the United States. Among their friends, the couple were teased as the "Hagar" and "Helga" of the Norwegian cartoon. Hagar, a Lutheran, had great respect for prayer and found the Bible to be a source of encouragement.

One day, Hagar had a spell and fell unconscious to the floor. A well-meaning neighbor dialed 911 and within minutes both the police and rescue squad arrived to whisk Hagar away to a hospital. Undoubtedly, he would be put on life supports, contrary to his wishes to remain at home and "let nature take its course." His wife stood guard over her unconscious husband, challenging both law enforcement officers and EMTs until a hospice nurse appeared to validate Hagar's "Do Not Resuscitate" wishes. In time, Hagar regained consciousness, however, and actually lived for three more years!

Wishing to affirm the courage and steadfast loyalty of

Hagar's wife Helga, a hospice nurse and the hospice chaplain arrived a few days later, each wearing a Viking hat. They unfurled a scroll and bestowed upon Helga "The Helga Award" for manifesting the Viking spirit in our contemporary world. The family was also given a small replica of a Viking ship. As death neared, Hagar became more fearful, likening his emotional turmoil to a ship at sea in a violent storm. Having listened to his trepidations, his spiritual caregiver wrote this prayer based on the biblical passage of Jesus' having calmed the waves of the sea (Matthew 8:22):

> *O Christ,*
> *so long asleep within my boat,*
> *though waves of anguish*
> *and helplessness*
> *ravage my life,*
> *I've not disturbed your soft slumber.*
>
> *Wind whipped and frightened,*
> *I've sought to fight the storm alone:*
> *a solitary battle for this fragile craft*
> *tossed from wave to wave*
> *as if for play*
> *until broken.*
>
> *Sinking amid*
> *Fierce waves*
> *With gnashed white teeth*
> *Threatening to devour*
> *At last*
> *I shout*
> *Not a moment too soon —*
> *O Christ awake.*
> *Save me!*

This prayer afforded Hagar great consolation and he died quite peacefully.

Spiritual Exercise

What waves tend to overwhelm you? Name them and then select one with which to "dialogue," i.e. carry on an imaginary conversation orally or in written form.

_____

_____

_____

_____

_____

_____

_____

_____

_____

_____

_____

_____

_____

The Man who Died Laughing

Jerome was a seventy-five-year-old former postman who was afflicted with pancreatic cancer. His prognosis was said to be only one or two days, so he opted to go home to die.

In familiar surroundings, however, he rallied, both emotionally and physically.

His children and grandchildren visited often and many hours were spent in their backyard garden. A parish priest also visited regularly

A man of faith, Jerome had no fear of dying. His humor appeared to spring from an inner fountain of joy. One evening, the family gathered about the bedside of Jerome and began to tell funny stories about him. He joined in uproarious laughter, sharing his own memories as well. His daughter, for example, recalled how she would come home from school to discover that her dad had dressed up the ducks in their yard in her dolls' clothes. Once more the family chuckled.

Then Jerome's son said, "Dad, remember the night we were walking through the snow on our way to Christmas midnight Mass at the Cathedral and we saw Santa Claus being thrown out of the Bottoms-Up Grill?" Jerome laughed and his children laughed, whereupon Jerome died with a big grin on his face.

Initially, the family was horror-stricken: "My God, we

laughed while our father died!" Later, however, they concluded that since Jerome lived surrounded by love and laughter, it
was more than appropriate that he die the same way.

Spiritual Exercise

Reflect on appropriate and inappropriate uses of humor in
your lived experience. What makes the difference?

It has been said that "as we live, so shall we die." Plan a
wake, funeral or memorial service reflective of your life.
Include meaningful music, symbols, values, readings, stories
and/or a life-review collage.

An alternative is to plan a celebration of life for an occasion such as a birthday. Guests may be asked to bring a
humorous or poignant memory, photos, or significant song to
share.

JOTTINGS: _____

_____

_____

_____

_____

_____

_____

_____

_____

_____

_____

_____

_____

_____

_____

_____

_____

_____

_____

_____

_____

_____

_____

_____

_____

_____

Relishing the Strawberries

L eo was a fifty-year-old man who had been diagnosed with a brain tumor. After numerous surgeries, chemotherapy and radiation, he was told by his physician, "There is nothing more we can do for you."

Depressed, Leo retired to his home where he refused to eat or interact with anyone. At the request of his parish priest, a hospice chaplain visited him and ascertained that Leo's depression was not so much related to impending death, but, rather, to remorse that he had failed to live.

As an automobile salesman, Leo had focused primarily on selling cars and making money. Little time remained for his family, two sisters who lived at a distance, or Marie, a friend whom he had never gotten around to marrying.

The chaplain shared with Leo a Zen story about a man being pursued by a ravenous tiger who chases him to the edge of a cliff. Fortunately, the man spies a vine which he quickly wraps around a tree. He lowers himself over the cliff out of the reach of the tiger, but then he spies the sharp rocks and crags below him. At the same time, a mouse begins to gnaw at the vine!

Suddenly, he sees a large strawberry growing out of the side of the cliff. He picks and eats it, smacking his lips and declaring, "That is the best strawberry I've ever eaten!" The moral of the story was then explained: how often, in life, we look back over perils of the past or focus on fear of the future rather than relishing the strawberries of the present moment.

Brightening, Leo took to heart the story and decided that although some of his choices were irrevocable by virtue of their being past, others were not. He proposed to Marie and the two were married at a small ceremony in his home. Gifts bestowed were those to be used to celebrate the present moment. One sister, for example, brought from her seaside home a cooler of lobsters for a picnic. Another arranged for a limousine to take the newlyweds wherever they chose to go.

Leo and his bride enjoyed quality of life for two months. When Leo finally died, surrounded by loved ones, he was peaceful and a much happier man.

Spiritual Exercise

Make a conscious effort to relish the strawberries of this day. A dab of strawberry aromatherapy oil on each hand or wrist may serve to remind you. At the end of the day, have a literal feast of strawberries while recalling blessings received.

Another option is the Native American ritual of the berry basket. Appropriate at Thanksgiving or other occasions of gratitude, a basket of berries is passed around a circle of family and friends; each person takes a berry and gives thanks for a blessing received.

BLESSINGS: _____

_____

_____

_____

A Leap from Faith

R oger was an elderly gentleman with a tumor on the carotid artery. Realistic about his disease and prognosis, he was simply waiting to die, and impatient with the process.

Although initially brusque and cryptic in his remarks, Roger grew to appreciate visits with the hospice staff, evidencing, if only transiently, cordiality with occasional flashes of humor. This proved to be a thin veneer, however, coating deep bitterness regarding both his life and his impending death.

To our dismay, one day, while alone, Roger leaped from a bridge and fell to a concrete pavement below. He had left behind a note in which he thanked his caregivers and family and absolved them of responsibility for his final act. Even so, the hospice staff remained fixated on the violence of the act, unable to understand or identify with such a course of action.

Subsequent dialogue, along with the following reflection heightened awareness of our own more subtle manifestations of violence and fear:

Roger,
your desperate leap
from a Gethsemane edifice of steel and stone
was far more than an agonized embodiment
of Jesus' prayer,
"Let this cup pass from me."
The shattering of your body

as bone hit bone
had reverberations in our hearts as well,
smashing illusions
and reducing to silence
the wall of words with which
we seek to surround ourselves.
Splinters of truth
more painful than swords
pierced our garments of nonchalance
rendering us naked and afraid:
afraid of our own loneliness and despair,
afraid of relationships which are dutiful tokens
rather than expressions of heartfelt love,
afraid of the lack of meaning in our own lives
and most of all afraid of a violence
more subtle and thus more deadly
than the path you chose:
the violence of our ideals and expectations,
the violence of non-forgiveness,
the violence of a tenacity which
refuses to let go of broken dreams
and painful memories,
the violence of an acquisitive spirit
which tries in vain to fill up
the emptiness of the human heart,
the violence of an activism which is
a mere masquerade for goodness.

Dearest Roger,
may you find in death
the peace which eluded you in life
and may we
bring peace
by making peace within.

Spiritual Exercise

Have you ever considered harming yourself? Who or what helped you? What did you learn from the experience?

Write a description or draw a picture of the "you" before and after you received help.

Write a description or draw a picture of the help you received.

DESCRIPTION: _____

_____

_____

_____

_____

_____

_____

_____

_____

_____

_____

_____

_____

_____

_____

DRAWINGS:

BEFORE

AFTER

Good Boy

William, a sixty-five year old orthopedic surgeon from England, had been diagnosed with chronic obstructive pulmonary disease. World-renowned for his professional expertise, he was guarded about his family history. Although the recipient of widespread public acclaim, he was privately self-disparaging.

As his personal story unfolded, William shared that he was the child of alcoholic parents and had been sent away to boarding school at the age of seven. Discipline was strictly enforced and he was often "caned," that is, beaten for minimal offenses. Returning home for occasional vacations, he was the recipient, also, of parental punishment, though the reason for the beatings remained obscure. Thus, William grew up thinking of himself as "bad," and projecting his self-hatred upon others.

Though initially slow to trust, William grew in his ability to share his vulnerability and, in time, he penned these words:

Reflections of a "Bad Boy"
I knew not the cause of my caning,
but that whipping
cut deep into my heart,
branding me with the name "Bad Boy."
So I proceeded to act out my naughtiness
in childlike ways,
later acquiring "man tools,"

then beat myself
with canes of guilt
and self-abnegation.
As years went by
I found other whipping boys
as well.
Using words as weapons
I punished them, too,
for phantom deeds of pseudo-darkness,
more imagined than real.
Until a feminine presence
came to me.
Her name was "Hospes"
meaning Healing Love.
She did not judge me
nor seek to take my cane away.
Instead, she saw
beyond the masks
to who I really was,
then gave to me
a name born of Truth:
"Good Boy."

Spiritual Exercise

There is a biblical story in which a man continually beats his faithful donkey until God gives the animal the voice to speak out against the injustice (Numbers 22:22-30). In a spirit of "sacred reverence," it has been suggested that the moral to the story is epitomized by the words "Stop beating your ass!" Reflect on your own experience of punitive measures, be they warranted or undeserved.

Write a letter protesting an injustice in your personal or professional life. Share it as appropriate.

_____

_____

_____

_____

_____

_____

_____

_____

_____

_____

_____

_____

_____

_____

_____

_____

_____

A Medal for Patty

P atty was a forty-five-year-old Irish school teacher who was afflicted with lung cancer, presumably due to excessive smoking. Reflecting on her family's history, Patty shared that when she was a child, a younger sibling had died of leukemia, a loss from which her mother never had recovered. After the death, an invisible but palpable pall hung over the household.

As is often the case, Patty, though but a child, blamed herself for being powerless to alleviate the familial pain. Consequently, by anesthetizing herself with alcohol, she spent most of her adult life in a semi-stupor.

Given a prognosis of only one year to live, Patty was startled into looking at her life with new awareness. She joined Alcoholics Anonymous, made amends for relational hurts, and embraced life with new gratitude. Though still terminally ill, she penned these words just before her death:

Why Me, Lord?

*So many people
remain in bondage. . .
Why am I
becoming more free?
Why me, Lord?*

*Clouds of sorrow
loom large
on the horizon of this world,*

yet so often
a single ray of sunshine
seeks and finds its way
into my heart.
Why me?

Thousands starve
for want of bread.
Yet I hunger not,
being fed each day
in limitless communion.

Friends die,
overcome by poisoned potions
of self-destruction
while I have learned
to drink deeply
of the chalice of life
finding it more
than enough
to intoxicate me.
Why me?

Forgotten God,
forgive my forgetting
and thank you
for re-membering me.

Patty died peacefully, clutching the medal commemorating her first year of sobriety. It was worth more to her than Olympic gold!

Spiritual Exercise

Use the space on the next page to design a medal to honor a major feat in your life, be it an external triumph or an internal victory.

What Color is the Other Side of Darkness? by Jean Roche, RSM

53

I Believe I Can Fly

An African-American woman in her late thirties, Carlotta was admitted to the hospice in-patient unit for terminal care. Diagnosed with both AIDS and a brain tumor, she appeared lucid, but was unable to speak or walk. The mother of three children, she had been estranged from her husband for ten years. Having learned of her illness, however, he had returned to the family pleading for forgiveness. "I was terrified of love," he confessed, seeking to explain his flight.

A touching reconciliation ensued. Subsequently, he was at Carlotta's bedside day and night. Both he and Carlotta were appreciative of prayer and valued the hymns continuously played in the room.

In time, a decision was reached to have Carlotta go home to die. She was discharged to an out-of-county hospice and we lost touch. A year later, the elevator door opened and, to our amazement, Carlotta stepped out. Thanking us for her care, she reported that not a trace of AIDS remained in her blood; neither did any vestige of her brain tumor remain.

Incredulous, we questioned her regarding the source of her amazing healing. In response, she merely reminded us of her favorite song which had been played repeatedly at her bedside: "I Believe I Can Fly."

Spiritual Exercise

Write your own creed — not a rote recitation of formal religious beliefs handed down by others, but, rather, tenets grounded in an inner knowing which resonate with the truth of your own lived experience.

_____

_____

_____

_____

_____

_____

_____

_____

_____

_____

_____

_____

_____

_____

Images of God

Myron was an artist admitted to the hospice inn for respite care. He brought with him an easel, paints and charcoals, transforming his room into a veritable art gallery. Day after day, he would labor over his artistic endeavors, committed, if not driven, to this ceaseless process of creation.

One day, a caregiver sought to evoke from him the motivation for this unswerving devotion to his artistry. He looked at her for some time in quiet contemplation. Then he explained, that according to his Jewish faith, God gives each of us a special gift and mission. The utilization of this talent, he continued, is our gift to the planet and the sole legacy which we leave behind. Commending him for the beauty of his work, the caregiver expressed concern, however, for the seeming eventuality that one day he would be unable to paint any longer. "I am wondering," she asked, "what that would be like for you?"

Silence ensued. He sat back in his chair, breathed deeply and proceeded to reflect on her question. Then, with a small smile and air of reassurance, he replied: "God said his name was mercy."

Spiritual Exercise

Reflect on your own images of God. You may wish to draw

with your non-dominant hand a childhood image.

What led you to this view?

How has your image of God changed? Find a symbol which resonates with your present perception of God (or as some might say, the Divine Energy which permeates all creation).

Draw the symbol or write a prayer to the God of your understanding.

SYMBOL:

PRAYER: _____

_____

_____

_____

_____

_____

_____

_____

_____

_____

_____

_____

_____

_____

_____

_____

_____

Reframing the Past

Jim was a priest who had been sexually abused as a child. The experience had led him to deep distrust and he'd sought refuge in the protection of his vow of celibacy. "Love hurts," he said, voicing his determination never to love or be loved.

Instead, he poured his energy into his ministry. Bright and creative, he became well known for his ability to inspire and motivate others. Few, if any, knew of his deep, existential loneliness.

Although admired by many, he was hyper-critical of himself. A sense of guilt and shame regarding his sexual history remained hidden in his heart. He also harbored both anger and sadness that his parents had failed to come to his aid. He reasoned that they had not cared enough to notice what was happening.

When afflicted with a terminal illness, Jim shared his story with his spiritual caregiver. In time, he came to the awareness that the pain of his childhood had led him to search deep within and discover inner resources of courage, creativity and spiritual power. A dialogue with his parents revealed their oblivion to Jim's childhood trauma. They begged his forgiveness for having focused on his lesser endowed siblings because he "had always seemed so independent."

Subsequently, Jim penned these words in his spiritual journal, reframing his own story:

Blood Upon the Snow

Blood upon the snow.
Innocence too soon meets Judas.
Sharp blade of steel

Drops
Swift as lightning
Guillotining trust.

Blood upon the snow.
Coal-black grief
Smudges
Pristine whiteness.
Childhood held captive,
Consigned to the cellar of fear.

Yet in darkness
Twigs of remembered love
Eons old,
Vague vestiges of glory,
Infinitesimal sparks of joy
Gathered into greatness
Formed a fire
Chasing phantoms into shadow,
Mere friendly ghosts
Dancing on cave walls.

Blood upon the snow.
Purity and passion co-mingled
Water into wine
Chalice of Fire.
Christ re-consecrated.

Spiritual Exercise

Write a poem, letter or story reframing the darkness of your life into light.

_____

_____

_____

_____

_____

_____

_____

_____

_____

_____

_____

_____

_____

_____

_____

_____

_____

Celebrating the Colors of our Lives

Harold was an Olympic bobsledder whose life was characterized by excitement and speed. Married, he had great devotion to his wife and five children. When diagnosed with bone cancer, however, his predominantly exuberant spirit plummeted. In addition, he was in considerable physical pain. Estrangement in the extended family was yet another cloud looming larger in the blue sky of consciousness. Thus the path of his life seemed suddenly on a downward slope.

Considerable time was spent in ministering to the patient's physical and emotional issues. The gamut of feelings from sadness and anger to despair was explored. The "if-only's" and "what if's" of Harold's life were processed in detail. The negativity increased, however, and there appeared to be no respite from the exclusive focus on darkness.

One day, a spiritual caregiver suggested that there was far more to Harold's life than his present pain. She invited the patient and family to join in a meditation, a veritable life review using the metaphor of color. It proved to be evocative of myriad memories.

The family was then invited to create a mandala (a Sanskrit word for an all-encompassing circle) of Harold's life. Though initially shy, armed with oil pastels, they soon entered into the project with great excitement and glee.

The patient himself drew six red hearts representing his love for his wife and five children. A daughter drew roller skates and a bicycle, recalling how her father had taught her to overcome fear and try to do new things. She added that she was counting on her dad's encouragement as she embarked upon her new career of teaching. Another daughter drew an abstract pink configuration, expressing gratitude for Harold's unfailing affirmation of her femininity. A son drew yellow, orange and blue fish, honoring experiences of fishing trips with his dad. Harold's parents drew a moon and stars, entrusting their son to the embrace of the creator. When completed, the mandala of collective, colorful memories was hung on the wall of the patient's room. All agreed that this magnificent creation helped to restore perspective. *See appendix for the meditation Celebrating the Colors of Our Lives.*

Spiritual Exercise

Create one or more mandalas of your life, including appropriate colors and textures as well as symbolic configurations and/or photographs. Practice in the circles provided on the next page.

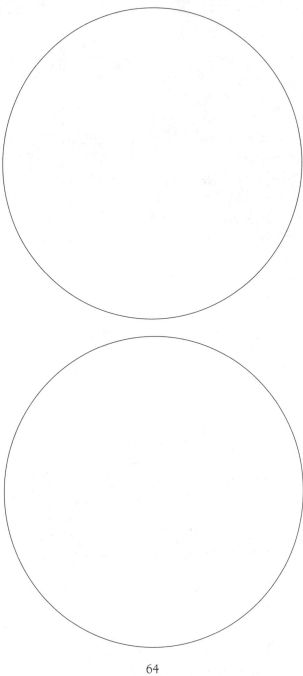

Lightening Up

D oris was of Russian descent, as was her husband who had died several years prior to her hospice admission. A nurse by profession, she was a "take charge" woman with a strong perfection ethic. Try as they might, her two devoted sons had never succeeded in measuring up to her expectations. She was equally ruthless in her own self-critique.

One day a chaplain shared with Doris the story of Balaam and the donkey from the Old Testament. It is an account of a master who severely beats his donkey without reason until the Lord gives the animal the voice to speak. "Why do you keep beating me?" he asks plaintively. "Haven't I done my best, always taking you where you wanted to go?"

Doris puzzled over the meaning of the story until she was told by the chaplain, "The moral of the story is this: Please, stop beating your ass!" Dorothy then laughed uproariously and, for a time, was more gentle with herself and others. Before long, however, she had reverted to past behaviors, resuming a hyper-critical stance.

It was decided to have a "stop beating your ass" ritual. Significant others in her life gathered with Doris to listen to the biblical story along with a poem on gentleness as well as appropriate music. A special "talking stick" was passed around. Participants, as they held the stick, spoke of the ways in which they had been harsh with themselves or with others. Then each one put down the stick and selected a feather from a multi-hued "bouquet." The delicate feather served as a symbol and reminder of tender mercy.

Throughout the remainder of Doris' illness, her feather remained prominently by her bedside. When she died, Doris' feather was placed in her coffin.

Spiritual Exercise

Spend a day being mindful of subtle manifestations of violence in your personal and professional life. Each time you detect a harsh or violent situation, offer a prayer for peace, sending healing energy to the persons involved.

JOTTINGS: _____

_____

_____

_____

_____

_____

_____

_____

_____

_____

The Woodcarver

Although advanced in years, Charles was a playful gentleman. Childlike, he reveled in games with his grandchildren and was described by his wife as "a big kid at heart." He kept a water pistol at his bedside and had been known to douse a hospice staff member in light-hearted jesting. At times, he was faced with "retaliation."

Once, a chaplain, armed with a similar "weapon," fired back, unaware that she was being observed by the Joint Commission of Hospital Accreditation! Fortunately for everyone, especially the chaplain, the accreditors recognized the good-natured intent of the exchange, so the hospice unit was not penalized.

Beneath the veneer of frivolity, however, Charles also had a wellspring of depth and spiritual wisdom. A woodcarver by profession, he continued his work while in hospice and surrounded himself with tiny figures of his own creation. Each of them was unique and most represented aged people.

Charles inspired both patients and staff by likening his creativity to that of God. He spoke of how lovingly he viewed each of his creations. If errors had been made in the carving process, they failed to obscure the beauty of the final product. "That's how God views our mistakes," he said, "and being a Master Craftsman, He continues to fashion and re-create us like a potter with clay."

What Color is the Other Side of Darkness? by Jean Roche, RSM

Spiritual Exercise

Buy some clay. While listening to quiet music, play with the clay, fashioning some creation, be it real or abstract. Below, reflect on what the process of shaping the clay was like for you.

REFLECTIONS: _____

_____

_____

_____

_____

_____

_____

_____

_____

_____

_____

_____

_____

_____

_____

Honoring Dr. Beaman

D r. Beaman was a general practitioner who lived in the neighborhood where I grew up. A kindly gentleman, perennially smoking a fragrant pipe, he had the uncanny gift of giving his full attention to each patient. Consequently, his front lawn sometimes resembled a picnic area, for patients would bring lawn chairs and a snack as they waited their turn. There was little impatience or animosity; rather, a festive atmosphere and the expectation of ultimately becoming the recipient of expert holistic care.

Years later, Dr. Beaman was diagnosed with a life-threatening kidney disease and I, a hospice chaplain, became his spiritual caregiver. Filled with conflicting emotions of dismay at his predicted demise and gratitude that I would have the opportunity of bestowing the mercy which I had first received from him, I began to visit on a regular basis.

Disclaiming religious connectedness, Dr. Beaman accepted his diagnosis with wry humor and equanimity. He did acknowledge, however, that he missed his boat trips on the Hudson River, his sole source of relaxation and transient escape from being constantly on-call for his patients and their families.

Consequently, his hospice home care nurse and I arranged a surprise trip to the Hudson River. It concluded with a feast of various pastas, champagne and Ben and Jerry's ice cream, his favorites.

Since Dr. Beaman was such a shy and humble man, I did not even attempt a gathering of grateful patients. Instead, I elicited from recipients of his care a collection of photos, cards and letters of affirmation which were subsequently arranged on a huge collage. His nurse and I incorporated the presentation into a ritual of affirmation. We reminded the doctor that the pipe for which he was so noted was the symbol of the healer in the Native American tradition. Thus we had decorated a peace pipe with medical memorabilia including a thermometer and hypodermic needle. Having filled the pipe with Edgewood tobacco, his favorite, we passed it around the assembled small group of family and hospice caregivers. Reminiscent of the smoke signals sent to the Great Spirit, each of us took a puff and expressed a hope, prayer or message of gratitude for this extraordinary man. Dr. Beaman was in awe of the collage and spent many hours pondering the messages of love and respect. I, in turn, felt grateful for the privilege of returning to him the gift which he had so gratuitously bestowed upon me and my family.

Spiritual Exercise
Create a collage of affirmation for a loved one or find a way to express your gratitude to a professional person who has served you in a special way.

JOTTINGS: _____

_____

_____

_____

_____

The Lion Who Learned to Purr

Patrick Lyons was a successful lawyer with a charismatic personality. Brilliant, he also had a childlike spirit of delight which was occasionally expressed in mischievous pranks, harmless in both nature and intent. His spirit of celebration was epitomized by his annual organization of a July 4th parade on the street where he lived. Among his proudest accomplishments was the establishment of a local baseball team.

Patrick was the father of two children. His son worked in child protective services and became a pioneer in creative educational projects in the state of New York. His daughter was an accomplished professional woman. Patrick's spouse was a glamorous, compassionate woman of Cherokee roots who was utterly devoted to her husband. All of them looked up to Patrick, generally acquiescing to his will as he had done to that of his now-deceased father.

A strong, traditional Catholic and active in the Hibernians, Patrick was proud of his lineage symbolized by his family crest featuring two lions. Numerous symbols of this animal adorned Patrick's home.

Upon being diagnosed with lung cancer, Patrick became increasingly volatile, roaring at his family over seemingly inconsequential issues. His wife and children tended to cower and placate rather than confront him, fearful of further enraging him. Increased episodes of shortness of breath heightened the tension for both the patient and his family.

Inspired by the situation, Patrick's spiritual caregiver wrote a children's story called "The Lion Who Learned to Purr." It was about the king of the jungle who was wounded and who pushed away his lioness and two cubs because he was so afraid. As the king became weaker, he allowed others to come close, relaxed and began to purr.

Surprisingly, Patrick loved this illustrated storybook. He had copies made for his family and friends. The metaphor helped both Patrick and his family relax and face his death together.

Spiritual Exercise

With what animal do you most identify? Write a children's story about a segment of your life using this imagery.

_____

_____

_____

_____

_____

_____

_____

_____

_____

_____

_____

_____

_____

_____

_____

_____

_____

_____

_____

_____

_____

_____

_____

_____

_____

Roots

J erry was a late admission to the hospice and was immi-
nently dying when the staff nurse and chaplain arrived at
his home. In respiratory distress, Jerry was surrounded
by his wife and five sons. Medication was given to calm him
and to alleviate his physical symptoms.

Subsequently, the family was encouraged to share stories
about Jerry. He was lucid, but weak and so merely listened. A
good dad, Jerry had coached his boys in Little League and
was often present to them when at home. A deacon in the
Lutheran Church, he valued prayer and the family joined in
intercessory prayer for his comfort and peace. Each family
member then spoke words of appreciation and gratitude. One
son asked his dad's forgiveness for falling short of his dad's
expectations.

After a period of silence, the family shared a picture of
Jerry in a kilt, explaining how devoted he was to his Scottish
roots. "He played his bagpipes every year at the Scottish
Games," his wife explained. *Amazing Grace* was his favorite
song. Since the family had a tape of Jerry playing this song,
they played it. Jerry's respirations, which had been so labored,
became peaceful. As the melody played, Jerry slowly looked
at the faces of his family, one by one, as if to etch each one
forever on the tablet of his memory. Then, he closed his eyes
and, as the last notes of the hymn sounded, Jerry died.

Spiritual Exercise

Draw or construct your own family tree, including symbols of cultural, professional, religious or spiritual meaning.

Celebrating our Brother Tony

Tony was a twenty-six-year-old man with a tumor on his carotid artery. Originally from Ohio, he had moved to Albany with his wife Helen. Married for five years, they had no children. Having been given a prognosis of two weeks, Tony also had been told by his doctor that he would most likely bleed to death. "It will happen quickly," he reported as if to reassure himself.

During the last days of Tony's life, his parents, five siblings, their spouses and children moved into the hospice in-patient unit. They literally camped out in the community room with sleeping bags, food, and toys for the children, all of whom were under five years old.

Tony's condition was known to all and openly discussed. His family learned to suction him when he had minor bleeding episodes and would joyfully exclaim when extricating a clot as if they were catching a fish!

There were tearful and fearful moments also. But most of the time both Tony and his family expressed their gratitude for the gift of life by living fully the present moment. Tony was the proxy godfather for the baptism of his newborn nephew. A surprise birthday party was held for Tony's eighteen-year-old brother with ice cream and cake for all. Tony and Helen perused the pages of their wedding album and kept their wedding candle burning continually. Prayer services and blessings were often offered at Tony's bedside.

One day, Tony's brother Joe whipped out his guitar and began a spontaneous ritual of celebration with a song he had written:

Celebrate Our Brother Tony

Many songs are written about
love, peace, the down and out.
People singing 'bout everything —
war, bills, just any old thing.

Changing times got us running around
jiving, working, plowing the ground,
sharing some time with one another.
Celebrate Tony, our brother.

Gather 'round — I want to say
a few kind things about Tony today.
I remember when he was small,
afraid of bees and things that crawl.
Celebrate Tony, our brother.

Gather 'round — I want to say
a few kind things about Tony today.
I remember writing some songs.
Tony got his typewriter and typed right along.
Celebrate Tony, our brother.

Gather 'round — I want to say
a few kind things about Tony today.
When he lived home it was neat as a pin.
Tony felt that dirt was a sin.
Celebrate Tony, our brother.

Gather 'round — I want to say
A few kind things about Tony today.
At his wedding to our surprise
Tony and Helen got cake in their eyes.
Celebrate Tony, our brother.

Gather 'round — I want to say
a few kind things about Tony today.
Add your memories to my song:

Then we'll all sing along.
Celebrate Tony, our brother.
Celebrate Tony, our brother.
Celebrate Tony, our brother.

— Printed with permission of Joe Mariotti

Family members joined in with many funny and loving affirmations that helped Tony to know how much he was loved. Tony continued to be celebrated long after his death which was swift and merciful.

Spiritual Exercise
Write a song, poem or letter celebrating the life and spirit of one of your loved ones; write one for yourself as well.

_____

_____

_____

_____

_____

_____

_____

_____

_____

_____

_____

_____

_____

_____

_____

_____

_____

_____

_____

_____

The Frog King

F reddie, a thirty-year-old Hispanic patient dying of AIDS, was admitted to the hospice inn for palliative care. Born in New York City, he had had a difficult childhood and was, as a mere youngster, exposed to crime, violence and drugs. For many years he lived under a cloud of despair and addiction to heroin.

When he met and fell in love with a soulful and spirited young woman, Yvonne, Freddie experienced a radical transformation. At last, he had a reason to live. He subsequently embarked on a journey of healing, freedom and peace.

The couple married and had two children, ages three and four. Freddie was filled with exuberance and joy, wasting not a moment of his new life. On a rainy day, for example, he would grab Yvonne's hand, run outside and merrily dance, heedless of the torrential downpour, so happy was he to be alive.

The diagnosis of AIDS came as a cruel and unexpected blow. After a period of mourning, however, Freddie's spirit was renewed and he resolved to cherish the life which yet remained to him. His hospice room was filled with love and laughter.

Among the meaningful symbols in Freddie's life was that of the frog. A sign on the door of his room affirmed that he was "The Frog King" and a huge frog puppet reigned in regal splendor. This became the theme of a ritual celebrating Freddie's life.

The ceremony began with a reading from the fairy tale The Frog Prince; that the theme of the transforming power of love echoed that of Freddie's life was clear to all. The following poem was then shared, accompanied by a tape of "Frog Music":

> *"Come here, little frog," said God to me.*
> *"But why," said I,*
> *"for no longer a tadpole,*
> *I am free to jump*
> *from lily pad to lily pad,*
> *or rest languid in the sun.*
> *I have arrived," said I.*

> *"Come here, little frog," said God to me.*
> *"But why," said I,*
> *"I am at home in oozy mud*
> *The rustle of the reeds is music to my ears*
> *and how I love to dine on feasts of bugs*
> *which skip about the surface of my pond.*
> *I have arrived," said I.*

> *"Come here, little frog," said God to me.*
> *"But why," said I*
> *"The rim of this pond is the boundary of my world;*
> *the fish are my companions,*
> *I can go no farther . . . .*
> *I am afraid."*

> *"Come here, little frog," said God to me.*

> *"JUMP!"*

Subsequently, participants in the ritual, including Freddie, his family, other patients and staff were given "frog cards" on which they wrote a phrase indicating what they wanted to jump from and toward.

These were then shared, e.g.

from fear to trust

from darkness to light

from rebellion to acceptance

from turmoil to peace.

Characteristically humorous, Freddie stated he wanted to jump from loneliness into the arms of his wife, Yvonne. The ritual concluded with Freddie dancing to the Pointer sisters' song, "Jump." Soon many others joined in the melee.

Weeks later, as we gathered about Freddie's bedside and he was close to death, we prayed: "Freddie, may you trust enough to jump into the Divine Embrace." And so he did.

Spiritual Exercise

Reflecting on your own life, recall experiences of personal transformation. Share these with another person or write about them below.

JOTTINGS: _____

_____

_____

_____

_____

_____

_____

_____

_____

_____

_____

_____

_____

_____

_____

_____

_____

_____

_____

_____

_____

_____

_____

_____

_____

Spiritual Transformation

Gerry was a sixty five year old woman admitted to hospice for palliative care. She had suffered several strokes secondary to her disease of polycythemia, a bone marrow disease in which there is an aberrational growth of blood cells.

An artistic, intellectual, and spiritually evolved woman, Gerry had no fear of death; rather, she believed our time on earth is to be one of learning lessons and becoming enlightened. Thus she viewed her illness as symbolically significant and often prayed for deeper understanding. On one occasion she shared this excerpt from her journal:

Sickness is
a series of painful
contractions
in the birth
of the Transformed Self.

One night, she had a brief but powerful dream in which a fox had been held captive in a cage for a very long time. Eventually, it became weak and wan, a grey ghost of its former self. The keeper of the cage decided that perhaps it was safe to release the animal. Still cautious, however, on opening the cage, she put a leash around the neck of the fox. To her surprise, on exiting the cage, the animal was suddenly transformed into a healthy, bushy-tailed red fox which ran away heading toward a purple mountain top.

Gerry treasured that dream, often sharing it with her care-givers in an attempt to "unwrap the gift" which the dream presented. As dream analysts had pointed out that each symbol in a dream represents a part of the self, she concluded that she was both prison and prisoner. She was the cage, the keeper and the fox.

Reviewing her life, she recounted a familial history of religious rigidity. Passion and creativity were matters of distrust rather than celebration. In spite of her intellectual enlightenment, Gerry was sexually repressed and had never integrated her more earthy, human self with the enlightened being she aspired to be. She saw the release of the red fox running toward the purple mountain as a symbol of the unity of earth and heaven, as well as the connectedness of disperate parts of the self. In energy, medicine, she explained, the color red represents the root chakra, connectedness to the earth whereas purple, the crown chakra represents relationship to the Divine. For Gerry, the dream was one of integration, heralding the most salient lesson of her life as well as the destination of her earthly sojourn. She believed that the final lesson of her spiritual life was that of embracing rather than denying her humanity.

As a means of reverencing the gift of the dream, she was given a stuffed animal, a red fox, which she embraced both literally and figuratively, as she lay dying, peaceful at last.

Spiritual Exercise

If you had the fox dream, what would it mean to you?

Name the bars of your cage, i.e. those attitudes, behaviors or observational beliefs which have held captive your more creative, exuberant spiritual self.

With what animal do you most identify? Write a prayer

from the perspective of that animal. Prayer of the: _____ .

_____

_____

_____

_____

_____

_____

_____

_____

_____

_____

_____

_____

_____

_____

_____

_____

A Rose for Teresa

Teresa was a gentle, loving woman with five children. Her husband, an abusive alcoholic, was often unfaithful. When Teresa was admitted to the in-patient hospice unit with end stage lung cancer, the sad saga of the family unfolded.

The couple had lost two children in death; one hit by a car and the other, a victim of leukemia. One of the surviving children had been entrusted with the responsibility of watching over his brother, Timmy, and was dismayed when the younger child ran out onto a busy street and was killed. His father had always blamed him for the death, withholding affection; his mother labeled him "careless", an epithet which he proceeded to live out in adulthood.

During the hospice family meeting, each member shared for the first time the emotions held captive in the heart for so many years. Copious tears were shed over the losses of a lifetime. Forgiveness was bestowed and received in gratitude. The culmination of this sacred experience occurred when Teresa's husband Tom broke down and shared his childhood history of physical, emotional and sexual abuse. He begged for the forgiveness of his wife and children, explaining that the anger so often directed at them was, in reality, related to his own past and the fact that his parents had failed to protect him from harm. A poignant exchange of forgiveness ensued.

The last "chapter" of this story was "written" later that day when Teresa confided her belief that all the suffering of her life was God's punishment because she had failed to follow the vocation of becoming a nun. Elaborating, the patient explained that as a young woman she had felt called to religious life and had asked for a sign of confirmation. Shortly thereafter, she received a rose which she viewed as divine affirmation of her discernment. Nevertheless, she had "turned her back on God" and married instead.

Aghast that Teresa viewed her suffering as punitive, a spiritual director said to her that the path of each of our lives is strewn with many roses, i.e. choices which God leaves us free to make. This spiritual guide shared her belief that the rose which Teresa had chosen had many thorns; yet she had clung to it in fidelity, holding the family together with her unconditional love.

On hearing her story reframed, Teresa burst into tears and said, "I have been waiting a lifetime for those words of absolution." Reflecting on the healing which had ensued after the family meeting helped Teresa let go of her "guilt" and come to believe that she had indeed fulfilled her mission on this earth. The spiritual freedom found in letting go of guilt was ritualized when, just prior to her death, Teresa expressed the wish to visit her home one more time. Though it was late November, she discovered to her surprise a solitary, gargantuan rose blooming in splendor on her front lawn. In awe, she brought the rose back to the hospice, instructing her family to press and preserve the petals, distributing them to each family member with her picture after her death. It was her hope that they might remember the lesson of the rose and continue to be open to giving and receiving forgiveness.

Spiritual Exercise

Reflect on an issue of forgiveness in your own life.

What is preventing you from moving toward reconciliation?

What would it take for you to forgive yourself or another?

Write a letter of forgiveness of yourself or another.

_____

_____

_____

_____

_____

_____

_____

_____

_____

_____

_____

_____

_____

The Might of the Horses

The meaningfulness of imagery in the spiritual life was highlighted by Herbert, an equestrian admitted to the hospice inn for palliative care. As the concrete image is symbolic of the spiritual fact, so was the centrality of horses paramount in Herbert's life.

Initially shy and extremely reticent on the first visit of the hospice chaplain, the patient acknowledged his discomfort, stating "I don't know what to talk about; I'm not a religious person." That connectedness to a formal religious tradition was not a prerequisite for a chaplain's visit was pointed out. Subsequently, Herbert was encouraged to talk about what *had* been most meaningful in his life.

He became enlivened as he spoke of his devotion to horses, dating back to childhood when he often went horseback riding. The interest continued through adulthood and Herbert developed a flourishing horse and carriage business for occasions including weddings and, yes, funerals, for he had access to a horse drawn hearse! Thus, the first prayer I shared with Herbert was one written by our Bereavement Coordinator, Eileen Clinton.

Prayer of the Horse

Lord, like the horse, grant me the ability to jump gracefully
over the hurdles that cross my path, the
stamina to run the most important races in my life,

but also to know when to stop running and at the
same time allow me to retain the natural beauty you
have blessed me with. I have carried many people
on my back and sometimes I need to rest.
Lord, help me to recognize when the time is here
to enjoy the simplicity of the green grass and
open pastures.
Amen

Reprinted with permission of Eileen Clinton.

Herbert was delighted and awed by the prayer and began to open like a springtime flower in the morning sun. The reading also provided a springboard for the patient's recounting of the hurdles in his life and the responsibilities which he had carried. Familial concerns which weighed heavy on his heart were shared as well.

Our sessions continued, and providentially, the book *Prayers from the Ark* provided a horse poem for practically every emotion with which Herbert struggled! On one occasion, for example, he shared a bevy of fears related both to himself and to his family. We concluded our session with the prayer of the fearful foal pleading for a divine response to his plaintive whinny.

As death neared, Herbert became less fearful and began to view his demise as a blessed release. Again, the prayer of the weary old horse whose coat was tattered embodied Herbert's own hope that the God of mercy would grant him a peaceful death.

Herbert's funeral included a multi-colored candlelighting ritual in which participants expressed gratitude and prayers by lighting candles from a magnificent central candle in the shape of a horse. His eulogy concluded with a reminder that in the Native American traditiion, the horse is a symbol of spiritual power. The following reflection was subsequently shared:

And now,
astride his mighty steed,
Herb soars over meadow and mountain,
bidding a final farewell to earth
as he gallops toward Home.

One might have thought that was the end of the horse imagery, but to my surprise, on the day of the funeral, Herbert's casket arrived in a carriage drawn by his very own horses. It was quite a spectacular event, including my blessing of the horses in the cemetery (an unforeseen and spontaneous alteration of the job description of the hospice chaplain) which was covered by three local television channels.

Spiritual Exercise

Choose a symbol which has been significant in your own life. Ponder its meaning. Draw it or find another way of honoring it and remembering its significance.

The Beggar's Bowl

Julie, a married woman with five children, was a hospice home care patient diagnosed with congestive heart failure. Nicknamed "Super Mom" by her husband and children, she was also active in her church, civic community and a local nursing home. More comfortable with giving than receiving, Julie found her escalating dependence on others excruciating. She was angry at her body for being unable to accede to her wish to remain active.

One evening she broke down and sobbed over the loss of control which was becoming more evident. Reflecting on the roots of her perfection ethic, she disclosed that her father was a tailor who had sought to "tailor" his children to his own precise and, in retrospect, rigid standards. Failure to measure up, even in trivial matters, was anathema; flaws of any kind were unacceptable. Thus Julie devoted her entire life to becoming the caregiver *par excellence*. Her own needs were neglected; indeed, she was not even cognizant of the needs of her body or spirit, exhausting herself on behalf of others. One day, she wrote these words in her journal:

> *I sought to tailor myself*
> *to meet your needs;*
> *thus you emerged*
> *well healed and souled*
> *While I, threadbare,*
> *grew blind to the Beggar*
> *in the street*

> *reaching out*
> *with plaintive eye*
> *and empty bowl*
> *for a single,*
> *golden glance of recognition.*

A hospice staff member, on reading the poem, placed a blessing bowl at Julie's bedside. Visitors were encouraged to write a message of gratitude, words of affirmation or prayer for Julie. In time, she came to appreciate the blessings she received, accepting her physical deprivations with greater equanimity.

Spiritual Exercise

To what extent do you identify with Julie's poem? Why or why not?

Create a blessing bowl for yourself using one-word blessings written on cards. Take one each day e.g. gratitude, courage, trust, serenity, openness, patience, inspiration, creativity, wonder and delight.

Plan and implement a ritual of affirmation for someone you know who seems overlooked.

JOTTINGS: _____

_____

_____

_____

_____

_____

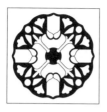

Kaleidoscope of Life

E lizabeth was a seventy-five year old single woman afflicted with colon cancer; her prognosis was two to three months. An affable woman with a kindly nature, she was well supported by the people on the street where she lived. Her sister visited often from New York City and a neighbor, Susan, was both friend and primary caregiver. Although Elizabeth had a male friend for thirty years, she opted not to marry preferring "companionship without the complication of deeper intimacy". Her love of children was channeled into her work, for she taught first grade for thirty-five years. Her support system included a community of public school teachers with whom she had been associated both personally and professionally. We arranged a reunion with some of her former students, including Dr. Anthony Tartaglia, now an internationally known hematologist.

Graced with a ready wit and the gift of spontaneous humor, Elizabeth collected jokes and cartoons. She took great delight in sharing them with others. Possessing a keen intellect, she was an avid fan of the television game show Jeopardy, competing with other hospice home care patients who shared their scores at the end of each week.

On a whim, I contacted Alex Trebek, the facilitator of the show, informing him of the joy his program was bringing to a group of terminally ill patients; I listed their names in valida-

tion. To my surprise, he mailed me six personally auto-
graphed photographs of himself. Elizabeth hung hers proudly
above her television set. She accepted both the light and
shadow of her life with serenity, informing me that "Life is
like a kaleidoscope: one turn and you get a whole new picture."

Before Elizabeth died, her friends and neighbors organized
a surprise party. Participants brought humorous stories to
share. A memory book was created consisting of photographs, poems, jokes and special stories. Hors d'oeuvres and
cocktails completed the celebration. Elizabeth was profuse in
her expression of gratitude, thanking her guests for helping
her to celebrate life in the moment, rather than "dwelling on
death."

Spiritual Exercise

Recall a humorous experience of your life. Share it with
another person.

JOTTINGS: _____

_____

_____

_____

_____

_____

_____

A Wish Fulfilled

Frank was the son of a wealthy Massachusetts family, who until the depression, enjoyed a life of opulence and affluence. A sumptuous mansion and high-end life style characterized their lives. The crash of the stock market, however, was a devastating blow to the family. Virtually destitute, Frank's father was faced with having to get rid of the dozen or so horses which had brought such joy to his son. Since he could not bear to give them away, he had them put to death.

Devastated, Frank, then sixteen years old, never rode again. Years went by. He grew up, married and had a family, including a devoted son, Jim. When diagnosed with lung cancer, Frank became a hospice home care patient and fully participated in our day care program, including weekly spiritual rituals, lakeside retreats, bingo games and delicious lunches cooked by hospice volunteers.

During one of these gatherings, a life review meditation evoked memories of Frank's personal history. Wistfully, he spoke nostalgically of the joy he had found in horseback riding. Our hospice Bereavement Coordinator, an enthusiastic equestrian herself, arranged a special outing for Frank. Back in the saddle again, the patient found the experience a reminder that it is never too late to reclaim joy and celebrate life!

Spiritual Exercise

Recall the joys of your own childhood, revisiting them literally or figuratively, engaging all of your senses of sight, sound, taste and touch.

An Early Christmas

Joan Mary was a fifty-two year old competent, brilliant woman who prior to her diagnosis of pancreatic cancer had an upper-echelon position in the State Department of New York. Childless, she had a devoted husband, Mark, and a bevy of personal friends as well as professional colleagues. When admitted to the hospice inn for palliative care, Joan Mary was realistic about her impending death and resolute regarding her goal for living fully the present moment. She also stated her desire to "draw nearer to God" and thus was receptive to the interventions of the hospice chaplain. She regularly attended weekly prayer services and rituals held in the community room.

One day, Joan Mary shared with the chaplain her love of Christmas. Her eyes filled with tears as the realization dawned that it was unlikely she would live until December 25. That she might, however, have an early Christmas, was suggested. Plans were immediately begun.

That evening the community room was decorated with Christmas ornaments and a tree brought from home. Her husband dressed up as Santa Claus, evoking gales of laughter when his pants fell down! Friends gathered about Joan Mary's bed placed in the center of the room and shared gifts as well as gratitude for the gift she had been in their lives. Many photos were taken, later displayed, in the patient's room. One, in particular, evoked awe and wonder; it was a photo of Joan Mary with an aura of light around her head.

After the Christmas party, ever in control, the patient decided she wanted to go home to die. Mark was delighted and we responded with alacrity, transferring her to hospice home care. By Christmas Eve, the patient was gravely ill, but hospice staff members came and gathered about her bed singing Christmas carols. When they departed, I was sitting next to Joan Mary on the side of the bed. She had just finished vomiting into the emesis basin which had become her constant companion. Gazing at me with watering eyes and an emaciated, jaundiced face, she stated, to my surprise, "Sister, I am just so grateful to God."

She proceeded to share a litany of gratitude that all that she had wished for herself had taken place: the celebration of Christmas, the desire to be at home, the longing to draw nearer to God. It was also her desire to bestow upon loved ones her most cherished possessions and Mark had spent hours labeling them lest he forget.

Joan Mary died the day after Christmas. Often I have reflected on her legacy to us, clearly one of gratitude. She was also an Incarnate Word of God to me, a reminder of the Scriptural adage: "I set before you life or death: Choose Life." She also taught me to seek to travel more lightly through life, divested not only of an excessive concern for material things but also free of the inner baggage which we so often carry.

Spiritual Exercise

Many of the gifts given Joan Mary were symbolic. Bestow upon a friend or family member a present symbolic of the gift he or she has been.

The Mayor of Room 5404

Z achary was a polite, self-contained gentleman admitted to a three-bed room at the hospice inn for palliative care of his end-stage cardiac disease. Instead of declining after admission, he seemed to thrive in the atmosphere of warmth, hospitality and tender, holistic care. As his roommates came and went, either due to death or discharge to another facility, he would welcome the newcomer and acclimate each person to his new surroundings.

In addition, he kept a faithful vigil over patients whose conditions had worsened, summoning a nurse or filling in physicians as they made their rounds. He sought to assuage anxiety, comfort the sorrowful, give hope to those in despair.

Having been affirmed for his role of merciful care, Zachary was reminded of his grandfather who had been mayor of a small municipality in the area. "He had a high hat and pocket watch," said Zach proudly, indicating that he had sought to follow in the footsteps of his grandpa being a source of compassionate care.

A surprise ritual of affirmation was subsequently planned by the hospice staff. Symbolic garb for the patient was purchased, including high hat and pocket watch. Michael Breslin, Albany County Executive, presented a proclamation honoring the patient. A large cake with appropriate designs and the acclamation "Honoring the Mayor of Room 5404," was then shared by all.

Spiritual Exercise

As the mystic Eckhart says, "If the only prayer you ever say in your whole life is 'thank you,' it would suffice." Write a letter of gratitude to a local or national leader.

_____

_____

_____

_____

_____

_____

_____

_____

_____

_____

_____

_____

_____

_____

_____

Embracing Vulnerability

As hospice became better known for its essential mission of life-enhancement and psycho-spiritual as well as medical care, our admissions increased and the over-extended interdisciplinary staff was becoming frazzled. Thus we welcomed medical student interns and were delighted when a fourth year resident in psychiatry opted for a hospice experience.

Upon his arrival, Albert was welcomed with open arms. Oblivious to the folly of the unaffirmed assumption, we envisioned him as being a great help to us. Before long, however, it became apparent that Albert was virtually immobilized by fear of being with a dying patient. He required a great deal of empathetic support himself. I witnessed a change of attitude among staff members. Uncharacteristically impatient, they expressed resentment, even anger toward Albert. I witnessed this tableau unfolding before me quietly, simply observing both subtle and blatant manifestations of an attitudinal shift.

One morning this reflection came to me, virtually creating itself as I penned the following parable upon the pages of my journal:

A Parable

Once upon a time, in the kingdom of healing love, there lived a group of great healers. With tenderness and mercy, they ministered to persons close to death. On wings of others' praise, their reputation spread quickly throughout the kingdom.

One day, a new healer, Albert, came into their midst. They welcomed him with open arms. As time went on, however, the warmth of the healers toward Albert cooled. For he was afraid of death and voiced his fear; he was weak and did not hide his vulnerability. So one by one, they turned on him. With barbs of words, they pierced his tender flesh or separated themselves from him by walls of silence.

When at last Albert departed from their midst, the healers breathed a sigh of great relief. They resumed their ministry to persons close to death. On wings of others' praise, their reputations continued to spread throughout the kingdom. And they remained oblivious to the fact that they had missed Albert, the Christ sent to save them.

Startled by the parable, the staff embarked upon a soul-searching reflection, humbly acknowledging their own fears and vulnerabilities which they had sought to banish from consciousness by pushing Albert away.

Spiritual Exercise
Write a parable expressive of a central lesson of your life.

_____

_____

_____

_____

_____

_____

_____

_____

_____

_____

_____

_____

_____

_____

_____

_____

_____

_____

_____

_____

_____

_____

_____

_____

_____

The Ball of Fear

Robert was a veteran of World War II and served under General Patton. A Lutheran, he had great devotion to the Bible and was able to recite the psalms by heart. His son, a Vietnam veteran, kept a faithful vigil; with dark eyes like a double-barreled shotgun, he crouched by his father's bed as if in a foxhole. The imminence of his dad's death evoked painful memories of his buddies killed during the war; thus he received special counseling for traumatic grief.

A polite, reticent man, Robert said little about his death, preferring to focus on topics which were less emotionally laden. One day, however, he began to reminisce about his military career. Assigned to the front lines, he was forbidden to use a gun lest his presence be discovered. Instead, his weapon was a garotte. In graphic detail, he described what it was like to kill a man in hand-to-hand combat. "There was always a ball of fear in my stomach," he said, stating that General Patton was as frightening to him as the enemy because he was "excessively punitive."

When Robert concluded his veritable military life review, the analogy of the war he was waging against cancer was gently introduced. "Yes!" he replied with vehemence. "The ball of fear is back and the weapons of chemotherapy and radiation are useless... I am without defense," he continued tearfully.

All the pent up grief of a lifetime poured forth and he sobbed for some time. A lengthy silence ensued. Then, sensing the timing was right, a spiritual caregiver began a slow recitation of lines from Robert's favorite Psalms: "God is my rock and my defense . . my fortress . . God will not leave me to face my enemies alone. . ." Later, Robert thanked her for the reminder, adding, "I almost forgot."

Spiritual Exercise

Reach out to a veteran or spend some time with the family of a man or woman serving in Iraq, offering emotional, spiritual or financial support. Write about the experience.

_____

_____

_____

_____

_____

_____

_____

_____

_____

Creating Sacred Space

J ames and Jenny were a devoted couple married for fifty years. Childless, they were deeply in love and devoted to one another. A successful businessman, James retired after having been diagnosed with lung cancer. In lieu of focusing on the dire prognosis, the couple resolved to express their gratitude for the gift of life by relishing the present moment. They took numerous trips to their favorite ocean location, walking hand-in-hand on the beach, collecting shells and spending hours simply being mesmerized by the ebb and flow of powerful ocean waves.

As time went on, however, James became much weaker, necessitating the cancellation of a long anticipated ocean excursion. Undaunted, Jenny decided to surprise her spouse by re-creating in their own home the delights inherent in their ocean excursions.

On the sun-splashed second floor landing of their home, she set up a table with their most exquisite silver and china. The centerpiece of the table was a huge Waterford crystal bowl filled with sand and seashells of myriad size and color. Scented candles of ocean air wafted in the gentle breeze, while a tape of classical music included the sounds of waves and seagulls. The menu consisted of shrimp cocktail and lob-ster tails, their favorite seaside cuisine.

Later, the couple snuggled together beneath a downy New

England quilt, watching a video of ocean waves on their large television screen. Jokingly, James remarked that it was the best ocean vacation he had ever had, adding with a twinkle in his eye, "I never even had to use my Visa card."

Spiritual Exercise

Create sacred space in your home, including meaningful symbols, objects from nature or key elements representative of earth, air, fire and water. List the things you plan to incorporate.

_____

_____

_____

_____

_____

_____

_____

_____

_____

_____

_____

Child of the Universe

Clarence was a seventy-five year old woodsman diagnosed with pancreatic cancer. Symptoms of pain and nausea were relatively well-controlled. Ambulatory, he had a prognosis of three months. Though a man of simplicity, Clarence had a brilliant mind and was essentially self-educated. He continued to be an avid reader during his stay at an area hospital.

The patient's father was German and a lumberjack; his mother, from Wales, wrote poetry. Both were deceased. Clarence always spoke fondly of his parents, accrediting them with his spiritual vision. Indeed, he viewed all of creation with eyes of childlike wonder and delight and was transported into near ecstasy by the aroma of pine trees or gazing at the immensity of the stars at night. Among the delights of his hospice sojourn was a pillow stuffed with pine needles and the opportunity of viewing shooting stars through a telescope on the hospital roof.

While often mindful of the creator, Clarence expressed doubt that God could spare a thought for him. "How could God have time for me," he pondered "when he is so busy with the artistry of the universe?" He expressed this thought without rancor. Philosophical about his illness, Clarence was graced with an inner peace and equanimity. He looked forward to his hospice visitors since he had no living relatives.

Neither did he have any friends or former co-workers in the immediate area. While Christian in terms of religious rootedness, Clarence found no meaning in formal religion connectedness. Content with worshipping God at the altar of creation, he described himself as "solitary, not lonely."

Reflecting on Clarence's belief that God was not mindful of him, I brought him a song entitled "You are Child." A musical variation of Psalm 8, it deeply touched Clarence with its reassuring message:

> You are a child of the universe,
> No less than the trees and the stars.

He listened to it often and we played it also at the hour of his death.

Spiritual Exercise

Spend some time gazing at the immensity of the stars, listen to the classical piece of music *The Heavens are Telling the Glory of God* by Franz Joseph Haydn, or read the book *Hymn of the Universe* by Teilhard de Chardin. Write about the experience.

_____

_____

_____

_____

_____

_____

_____

_____

_____

_____

_____

_____

_____

_____

_____

_____

_____

_____

_____

_____

_____

_____

_____

_____

_____

Phoenix Rising

Gloria was a Sister of Mercy who eschewed hospice care but was receptive to spiritual direction after her diagnosis of metastatic cancer. Fortified with 40 years of religious life, she was initially quite stoic, accepting her destiny with docility as "God's will."

A transforming event occurred, however, when the convent in which she had lived for decades caught fire and was virtually destroyed. It was as if those flames ravaged as well the wall of words with which she had sought to defend herself. Silence ensued.

Days later, I shared with her a guided meditation in the form of a religious life review, gently suggesting that she write about her thoughts and feelings. This was one of her entries:

> *"Dear God, as in my mind's eye I sift through the ashes of our*
> *ravaged convent, I ponder what has "gone up in smoke"*
> *for me over these many years ... persons who've*
> *died ... shattered illusions .. mere wisps of forsaken ideals .....*
> *old structures and ways of doing things .....*
> *charred remnants of time – honored traditions ...*
> *beliefs watered down by fire hoses of harsh*
> *reality .. In my heart, too, there lies this rubble and*
> *I continue to pick through these piles of soot-soaked refuse, hoping to find*
> *vestiges of what was – and still is – treasured.*

I sat with her as the gamut of repressed feelings emerged, found expression and were, in time, mercifully released: the unresolved grief over the death of her parents whom she had taken no time to mourn; the anger over mandated ministerial assignments inconsistent with her passion, personal preference and giftedness; the sadness over the dissolution of a close friendship; guilt over not having been "the perfect nun"; confusion over changes in the church; her fear of dying and doubts about God.

It was a painful but ultimately liberating experience of awareness; a dark night of the soul, in which she was stripped, empty. I was but a calm companion witnessing her story, validating emotions, only occasionally reminding her of Jesus' humanity, including his sadness, rage and terror. As she slowly journeyed through chaos to surrender to transformation, I shared with her the reframing of the story of the convent fire written by another Sister; it was based on the myth of the indomitable phoenix, rising unscathed from its nest of fire.

A Mercy Myth

On a warm summer evening,
shortly after the sun had touched with light
the outermost fringe of the western sky,
place of farewell,
a mystical bird, the phoenix,
circled with weary wings
over its nest of nurturance,
then slowly descended
upon its final resting place,
saddened by the imminence of fiery immolation,
yet taking pride in a mission completed,
Consumatum est.
tiny wisps of smoke,
scarcely discernible at first,
began the conflagration of the nest
which suddenly burst into flames
reaching greedily skyward

as if to seize and devour
all of heaven as well as the earth!
fingers of firelight traced grotesque
patterns of anguish upon the uplifted
faces of passersby.
silhouetted against the backdrop
of this nocturnal sun,
spirals of smoke – dark incense –
uttered a silent prayer
to the unseen God.
Baptism of Fire!
Painful Pentecost!
Refiner's flame
wherein all, save the essence,
is burned away.
suddenly, Waters of salvation
poured forth from all directions,
extinguishing the blaze.
in time, warm winds breathed softly
upon the black, sooted, sodden
piles of refuse.
on the third day,
noticed by but a few,
the ashes began to stir.
and lo, from their midst
emerged a tiny fledgling
with feathers of purple and red and gold –
a New Creation,
death having given birth
to the Spirit Child.
its name: Misericordia;
its spirit: that which
is boundless in us;
its home:
the temple of the universe
whose ceiling is studded with stars.

In time, Gloria found her faith rekindled. The culmination of this interior soujourn was epitomized by May Sarton's poem, *The Phoenix Again:*

115

On the ashes of this nest
Love wove with deathly fire
The phoenix takes its rest
Forgetting all desire

After the flame, a pause,
After the pain, rebirth ....

And one cold starry night
Whatever your belief
The phoenix will take flight
Over the seas of grief

To sing her thrilling song
To stars and waves and sky
For neither old nor young
The phoenix does not die.

Spiritual Exercise

Reflecting on your own experience of redemptive suffering, journal or create your own mythological version of how a moment of shattering became a moment of grace for you.

_____

_____

_____

_____

_____

_____

What Color is the Other Side of Darkness? by Jean Roche, RSM

_____

_____

_____

_____

_____

_____

_____

_____

_____

_____

_____

_____

_____

_____

_____

_____

The Way of the Cross

L ucy was a twelve year old child with leukemia. One of six children, she had a maturity beyond her years and was philosophical about her impending death. Often, she would sit in a rocking chair, holding her younger brother in her arms and talking to him about death. A devout Christian, she was certain of life after death and did not want her brother to be afraid.

Although Lucy remained at home throughout the duration of her illness, the family requested that she be allowed to die in the hospice inn. They did not want her siblings to have lingering memories or fears regarding her death in their home. Ironically, Lucy plummeted on Good Friday, the day of the Christian observance of the crucifixion of Christ. She was admitted to the inpatient unit accompanied by her parents and siblings. The patient was minimally responsive but appeared aware. To my surprise, her mother began to reflect on Lucy's life in the light of the Stations of the Cross. Just as Jesus was condemned to death, she said, her daughter's diagnosis was also a death sentence. Recalling that Christ stumbled beneath the weight of the cross, she noted Lucy's "ups and downs", both physical and emotional. In the Gospel account, Simon of Cyrene helped Jesus carry his cross and Veronica reached out in mercy to wipe his sweating brow. Similarly, Lucy's mom named the countless people who had come to her daughter's aid. The stripping of the garments of Christ was likened to the losses which Lucy had suffered: the loss of her hair, the loss of energy and vitality, the loss of her future and the loss of friends fearful of visiting because they didn't know what to do or say.

Lucy's mother concluded this mystical meandering with the conviction that as her daughter had participated in the suffering of Christ, so would she soon experience the joy of resurrection. Lucy died on Holy Saturday, the day noted for peace and merciful release.

Spiritual Exercise

The life of Christ, like our own, is a story of light and darkness, triumph and tragedy, love and betrayal. Choose an aspect with which you identify at this time and write a prayer.

_____

_____

_____

_____

_____

_____

_____

_____

The Revolving Door

C andy was a thirty year old young woman diagnosed with end-stage lupus. There had been an incredibly short interval between her initial diagnosis and the news that she was going to die soon. Yet, the young woman shifted gears with amazing alacrity, accepting her impending death with seeming serenity. She spent many hours seeking to console the incredulous family members and friends hovering anxiously about her bedside.

One day, she was asked by a spiritual caregiver what it had been like for her to receive such a dire prognosis. Sandy explained that she felt as if she were in a revolving door. Occasionally, she reported, it opened to reveal eternity, a place of peace and boundless freedom, inhabited by the spirits of those who had died. Reassured, yet cognizant that it was not yet time for her to exit, she witnessed the door closing. Subsequently, it opened anew to reveal loved ones gathered about her bed in the hospice inn.

One day, Candy was visited by her godmother, a woman who had been reluctant to come to the hospital where her child had died a few years before. As she stood trembling in the doorway of Candy's room, the patient looked up and exclaimed "Betty! You don't need to worry about Billy. I've seen him and he is safe and happy." A deluge of tears ensued. Shortly thereafter, the revolving door moved once more, opening to the broader spectrum which Candy had previously witnessed. It was time for her to exit. And so she did.

Spiritual Exercise
What is your vision of what lies beyond the grave? Describe it in a journal entry or drawing.

_____

_____

_____

_____

_____

_____

_____

_____

Vanquishing Demons

Pierre was a distinguished gentleman originally from France. Suave and well-mannered, he was intent on dying as he had lived, with dignity and grace. Equally committed to protecting his family from worry, he indicated that his diagnosis of metastatic colon cancer was "no big deal." He shrugged off expressions of concern, saying "We all have to die sometime."

The family reported, however, that Pierre's nights were "terrible." Asked to explain, they stated that he was up all night, seldom sleeping. When he, exhausted, finally fell asleep, he moaned and groaned, awakening in a cold sweat. When questioned, he denied there was a problem. *"De rien,"* he would say in his native language. It is nothing.

A spiritual caregiver was later able to engage the patient in dialogue regarding his difficult nights. He told her that he had recurring nightmares of being chased by devils. Further exploration led to the disclosure that Pierre was a Catholic who had divorced his first wife and remarried. Thus, he believed that when he died, he would "burn in hell." A visit from the parish priest assuaged Pierre's fears and his nightmares ceased.

Spiritual Exercise
Recall a nightmare you have had. Draw it. How did it relate to what was happening in your life at the time?

The Giveaway

Tim had been a robust laborer until he developed lung cancer and was eventually admitted to the hospice inn for palliative care. A former employee of a local meat packing company, he was well respected by those with whom he worked and deeply loved by his family.

A superb listener, he had a bevy of visitors. Though ill, he retained the gift of giving his full attention to each one, offering counsel or helping them discover the wisdom within.

One day he shared with me the story of a special relationship with a co-worker, Patrick, who had come to the company just out of high school. They had become good friends, bonded by their love and loyalty to their occupation. Hard work was a strong value for each. Heavily laden with the sadness of helping to care for his crippled mother, Patrick had opened his heart to Tim, finding consolation and support. But they had drifted apart after the meat packing company closed.

A touching reunion occurred when the young man was invited to a family meeting. Stories of the past, both light and shadow, were shared. Patrick was able to thank Tim for being a surrogate dad.

As death neared Tim became busy deciding to whom he would give his most treasured possessions. He was making a list to ensure that his wishes would be respected; there was a special significance and symbolic meaning to each gift. In lieu of simply including the rationale in a written will which would be read after his death, it was suggested that instead, Tim have a giveaway ceremony to personally express his sentiments to his loved ones. He responded to this idea with characteristic enthusiasm. Later, family and friends gathered in the community room of the hospice. A granddaughter played his favorite song on the piano; it was a veritable musical life review. Subsequently he bestowed his gifts, articulating the special meaning of each and why he had chosen the person who received it. Each felt especially blessed, for the value of each gift lay far beyond the material worth.

Spiritual Exercise

On a special occasion such as Thanksgiving or Christmas plan a giveaway ritual for family or close friends, or develop a practice of occasionally bestowing such a gift upon a loved one. Whom might you wish to include? What gifts would you choose to bestow?

_____

_____

_____

_____

_____

_____

What Color is the Other Side of Darkness? by Jean Roche, RSM

_____

_____

_____

_____

_____

_____

_____

_____

_____

_____

_____

_____

_____

_____

_____

_____

_____

This Is Your Life

Lizzie was a diminutive woman, seventy five years old. Lines etched upon her wizened face indicated a lifetime of suffering. When admitted to the hospice inn for end-of-life care, she was bitter and depressed.

Weeks of subsequent conversation evoked a history of disillusionment and disappointment. There was a ray of light, however: Lizzie became enlivened as she spoke of "the good old days" growing up in the south end of Albany. She mentioned the names of old friends from whom she had become distanced over the years.

Hospice staff members managed to contact a number of these former friends and arranged a surprise party for Lizzie. On the day of the event, the curtain was drawn around Lizzie's bed. The guests quietly assembled in a circle. In a quavering voice, one began the replay of memories. "Lizzie, she said, "do you remember how we used to play in Margaret Moran's cellar?" Astounded, Lizzie responded incredulously, playing a guessing game as to the identity of each speaker. Finally, the curtain was opened and Lizzie enjoyed beer and pretzels with her former playmates. Later she stated that it was the happiest day of her life.

Spiritual Exercise

Plan a surprise "This Is Your Life" celebration for a loved one.

_____

_____

_____

_____

_____

_____

_____

_____

_____

_____

_____

_____

_____

_____

_____

_____

_____

_____

_____

The Belly of the Whale

Stories, both personal and archetypal, have the power to heal. The mere recounting of one's personal story is itself therapeutic; in addition, it enables the listener to discern areas of the storyteller's life in need of reconciliation as well as those warranting celebration. Mindfulness of the connection with Greater Story, furthermore, broadens perspective and may evoke transformational insight. Thus our weekly spiritual gatherings sometimes focused on a myth or Bible story.

Such was the case when a children's version of the Biblical tale of Jonah and the Whale was presented. In simple language, the story of Jonah's flight from God, his having been thrown overboard and swallowed by a whale was told. It included his having been cast upon the shore, subsequently accomplishing the astounding feat of converting the Ninevites. Later, however, Jonah becomes obsessed with a withering "broom tree" which had offered him comfort.

The story was followed by a guided meditation inviting members of the group to "place" themselves somewhere in the story. Did they, like Jonah, feel thrown overboard or abandoned? Beset by waves of anger or sadness? Were they in the belly of the whale, place of darkness or incubation? Had they experienced surprising accomplishments – or an obsession blinding them to a broader perspective?

The group was then invited to draw a picture, journal or simply silently reflect on what the experience was like for them. Meaningful sharing ensued. One participant stated that she identified with Jonah's flight from God. Elaborating, she stated that throughout her life she had played hide and seek with God. Now she felt lost and prayed that God would find her. Others acknowledged feeling overwhelmed by waves of sadness, anger or depression. Another participant, a former high school English teacher, penned the following poem:

Chaos, a storm cloud-hued whale
reeking of briny, brackish sea water
swallows my Jonah-self,
plunging me into powerlessness:
pitch-black, impenetrable night, devoid of stars.
Like a captor, savior, mother,
the ponderous, paradoxical beast carries me safely
through churning, turbulent waters.
We are one, whale and I,
paradigm in warm womb of becoming.
Invisible light transforms, blesses, missions
as I am spat out once more upon the shore:
sent to help Neo-Ninevites shed their sackcloth of separation.

Yet another individual focused simply on the word "overboard" stating that she had always gone overboard in her life, working too much, worrying too much, eating and drinking too much. She acknowledged that she was a Libra, who in seeking to find balance, went from one extreme to another. The facilitator of the group, also a Libra, spontaneously recited an original poem:

Lithesome, leaping Libra
jumps from scale to scale
yet in her quest for balance
rarely peace prevails.
Skimming skyward like a bird

or plummeting to earth
The best of each eludes her, of
balance, she has a dearth.
Things are always black or white
or, good or bad, it seems
and oh! the energy expended
in going to these extremes.

Libra my child, please listen:
This malady needs no pill
If you're seeking to find balance,
you need only be still.

This evoked laughter from the group and seemed an apt moment to bring the ritual to closure.

Spiritual Exercise

Select a myth or Bible story with which you identify in some way. Find your place in the story. Draw or write about what the experience was like for you.

DRAW HERE:

What Color is the Other Side of Darkness? by Jean Roche, RSM

WRITE ABOUT YOUR EXPERIENCE: _____

_____

_____

_____

_____

_____

_____

_____

_____

_____

_____

_____

_____

_____

_____

_____

_____

_____

_____

Reclaiming Joy

Marty, a reclusive, introverted gentleman, was admitted to hospice home care after a diagnosis of end stage lung cancer. He lived in a virtual hovel of disarray and was surrounded by piles of magazines and an infinite variety of possessions ordered from a television marketing company. His sole companion was his dog, Wolf. Open cans of Dinty Moore stew on top of his stove lent tacit testimony to the nature of his culinary preferences.

Alone and with no living relatives, Marty had no friends. He recounted a sad story of having fallen in love with a woman who later deserted him for someone else. The incident eroded his sense of trust and he indicated that he preferred solitude to company. Christian in terms of religious rootedness, he stated his belief that God had put him "on hold."

As his condition declined, Marty's breathing became more labored and he was put on oxygen. His appetite waned and he declined offers of ham and cheese sandwiches and chocolate chip cookies, which had been his favorites. Asked what had brought him joy in life, Marty brightened visibly and with renewed energy recounted fishing trips on the Mohawk River. In vivid detail he described feeling the warmth of the sun on his face and the caress of a breeze. He never tired of watching the water, its ripples having had a mesmerizing effect of peace and relaxation. "Wolf was happy too in those days," he added.

One day, a hospice volunteer and I arrived at Marty's home with a fishing rod, bait and a picnic basket packed with the patient's favorite food. We informed him that our destination was the Mohawk River! Initially reticent, he stated that he did not feel able to make the trip, but upon being reminded that his favorite site was not that far away, he agreed to come. We also brought along a portable oxygen tank. Wolf was overcome with exuberance jumping into the car, out the window and back again.

It was a perfect day with an azure blue sky, low humidity and warm sun. Marty's eyes widened with wonder and pooled with tears as we arrived. Slowly acclimating himself to the scene, he breathed a long sigh and basked peacefully in the sun, supervising our feeble attempts at fishing. To our surprise, he removed the oxygen, stating he no longer needed it as he devoured two sandwiches and several cookies! Later, he spoke a spontaneous prayer of gratitude to God, the Creator, who, he decided, no longer had him "on hold."

Long after Marty returned to the cramped quarters and stale air of his tiny home, he carried the memory of the Mohawk River in his heart, readily responding to visualization of the scene.

Spiritual Exercise

Visit a favorite place in nature – or visualize it – using all of your senses of sight, sound, taste, and touch to be fully present. Describe or draw it on the next page.

DRAW OR PASTE A PHOTO HERE:

WRITE ABOUT YOUR EXPERIENCE: _____

_____

_____

_____

_____

_____

_____

_____

_____

_____

Tapestry of Life

Weekly rituals were integral to the psycho-spiritual care of our hospice program. Creative, evocative and spiritual, they focused on salient themes in the lives and hearts of our patients and their families. Members of the inter-disciplinary team and occasionally, even physicians attended.

One day, the theme was "Tapestry of Life." It included participants' selecting a square piece of cloth from among a variety of colors, textures and designs to which each felt drawn. A meditation based on identification with the material ensued. After a period of quiet reflection, the group was invited to share. I recall a familial caregiver selecting burlap and speaking about how frazzled and frayed she felt "around the edges." Yet, she observed, the greater portion of her life was intact. She expressed appreciation for the opportunity of voicing her fears and frustrations as well as having perspective restored.

Another patient had chosen lace. She commented on its loveliness but pointed out the pain of the process of becoming lace: the losses and vulnerabilities; the embarrassment of having to be dependent; the "cutting away" of what once seemed so essential.

A brocade with silver and golden threads against a dark background was the choice of a woman who shared both the light and shadow of her life. Denim was the choice of a construction worker. It was the garb of his life-time and he proceeded to share memories of his work. The stories were both humorous and reflective of pride in his accomplishments. He was grateful that he had provided well for his family, particularly their material needs.

It was amazing to witness what a small fabric evoked: the softness of velvet, the roughness of tweed, the grace of chiffon, the sultriness of silk – each found the voice to speak out, seeming to come from a deep place of soul.

When the sharing was completed, we attached each square to a piece of corkboard, creating a magnificent tapestry of myriad colors, textures and designs. We reverenced our collective creation with incense and lit a candle before it, gazing in wonder and silent contemplation.

The ritual was concluded with a simple, spontaneous prayer:

> *God of creation, we thank you*
> *for bringing us together,*
> *in this living tapestry*
> *of joy and sorrow*
> *turmoil and peace*
> *darkness and light*
> *May we re-member*
> *our connectedness*
> *with one another*
> *and with you*
> *Help us to be*
> *ever-mindful of our*
> *solidarity,*
> *both in suffering and*
> *in celebration,*
> *as we place our trust*
> *in you,*
> *the Master Craftsman*

Spiritual Exercise

Create a tapestry of your life, a collage of varied colors, textures and designs.

Write about it – or share it with another person.

_____

_____

_____

_____

_____

_____

_____

_____

_____

_____

_____

_____

_____

_____

_____

_____

_____

Hands

Weekly spiritual rituals at our hospice often focused on life review, assisting participants in identifying areas of life in need of reconciliation as well as those warranting celebration. An especially evocative meditation by Ed Farrell uses the symbol of hands to guide participants in reflecting on their lives, going back to the tiny hands of a newborn child. It includes a review of all their hands have done, from dressing and feeding themselves to the mastery of adult activities. The meditation refers also to emotions their hands have expressed, from anger, even violence, to tenderness and love; to gifts given and received.

Subsequent sharing invariably reflects a gamut of feelings and memories, both painful and poignant. Occasionally, the topic of sexual abuse emerges, enabling psycho-spiritual caregivers to address the issue further in a more private setting. More often, memories of a deceased loved one, a dear friend or forgotten accomplishments surface, evoking gratitude.

In one session, for example, a participant reflected on her mother's hands, all gnarled and crippled from rheumatoid arthritis; yet she managed to knit mittens for the poor. Thus the image of the crippled hand, rather than evoking dismay, was a source of inspiration, highlighting the indomitability of the human spirit. Some recalled the aged hands of grandparents many of whom had been surrogate moms or dads. The

139

delicate hands of a child, the rough hands of a dad who labored to support his family and the compassionate hands of a physician or caregiver were among the memories shared. When all had spoken, the following reflection, written by a family practice physician who also cares for hospice patients, was read:

Lessons from my Grandfather

With the eyes of a child, I saw you as a large man with big hands, usually covered in grease, who liked to "tinker" on cars and clocks. You taught me curiosity and the importance of asking "Why?" or "How?"

With the eyes of an adolescent, I saw you in the hospital and met people who said, "Your grandfather saved my life." You made me believe I could be a doctor also. You taught me the importance of education and perseverance.

With the eyes of a physician, I now see you were often more than a doctor. You were a healer. Your work went far beyond the operating room and touched the lives of your patients and their families. You taught me compassion and generosity.

With the eyes of an adult, I saw you grow old and more frail. I was still impressed by the size of your hands! The lessons continued, however. The mind was slowly being extinguished but never the spirit. You taught me to appreciate good health and love of life.

No matter what the age, my eyes were always looking up to you. The teacher may be gone but the lessons will live forever.

— *Sean P. Roche, MD*

The next part of the ritual varies. One option is to have participants massage the hands of one another with lavender lotion, an aroma associated with healing and harmony. Another involves the washing of hands from a large crystal bowl. A third alternative is that of passing a small crystal bowl of water around the group assembled in a circle, inviting each to bless the hands of the person seated to the right. An especially touching memory was one in which a patient's daughter was seated on the left and her physician on the right. The daughter blessed her mother's hands, thanking her for the gift of life and all the nurturing done by her hands. The patient then received the bowl of water and, with trembling hands, turned to bless the hands of her doctor. Eyes filled with tears, as she thanked him for all he had done, assured him of her conviction that he had done all he could to make her better, and expressed gratitude that he had not abandoned her but was remaining faithful to the end.

Spiritual Exercise

Spend some time reflecting on your own hands and all that they have done throughout your lifetime. Find a way of reverencing your hands, e.g. a massage, a symbolic adornment, a written or spoken message of gratitude.

_____

_____

_____

_____

_____

_____

_____

_____

_____

_____

Home for Good

L il was a strong woman, seasoned by pain and by prayer. Deserted by her husband when her five children were young, she had brought them to a local orphanage which she visited regularly. Meanwhile the children bonded as never before. Wistfully, they witnessed other children going "home for good," dreaming of the day when that would be true for them as well.

Needless to say, when that day finally came, there was great jubilation. As years went by, however, two of Lil's beloved sons died; one in military service and the second in hospice. It was around the bedside of the latter son, Bill, that we first met Lil and her three surviving children: the warm and compassionate Ann Marie, the soulful and debonair Simon and the feisty and spirited Mary Lou. Though the death of Bill at 45 was a sad one, he was surrounded by the love and laughter of this spectacular family. Their fidelity, faith and resilience, as well as the pathos of yet another loss, evoked the compassion and love of our staff.

Aware of the transiency of life and the precious gift of intimate relationships, this family manifested the ability to feel the joy of life and dance it; feel the the pain of life and weep. Other-directed, they frequently reached out to other hospice families, and expressed care and concern for the staff as well. At times, Mary Lou, a hairdresser, offered to cut the hair of staff members too busy to care for themselves!

When Lil was herself diagnosed with cancer and admitted to the hospice program, we felt we were caring for one of our own relatives. True to their ebullient spirit of devotion, the family rallied once more, ensuring that Lil enjoyed quality of life to the very end. Her unfaltering faith and inner strength enabled her to accept her dying with equanimity. When she finally died, her family and I prayed in gratitude that Lil was "Home for Good."

Sadly, a few years later, Mary Lou also died of cancer and was reunited with her mother and brothers . . . also Home for Good. The metaphorical moral to this story, the importance of coming home to the heart, is a spiritual legacy which remains with me still.

The story also calls to mind the words of Francis Thompson in his poem *The Hound of Heaven:*

> *All which I took from you,*
> *I did but take*
> *not for thy harms*
> *but just that thou might seek it*
> *in my arms.*

> *All which thy child's mistake*
> *fancies as lost,*
> *I have stored for thee at home.*

> *Rise, clasp my hand and come.*

Spiritual Exercise

Reflect on the place which you called home when you were a child. Engage in a life review by visiting each room of the house in your imagination. Draw a picture and/or write about what this experience was like for you. If it is the metaphorical message of the story which most resonates with you, you may wish to draw a picture of "the home of your heart," using colors and symbols revelatory of what lies within.

_____

_____

_____

_____

_____

_____

_____

_____

_____

_____

_____

_____

_____

_____

D<small>RAW</small> <small>HERE</small>:

Who is Sarah?

To the casual observer, Maureen and Jim seemed an ordinary couple. The parents of a five-year-old, Hannah, they were eagerly awaiting the birth of twins. The pregnancy went well until the eighth month when an ultra-sound test revealed that "Baby A" was unresponsive, the walls of her heart having thickened. An emergency C-section was done. A cardiologist told her parents that the child's heart was not contracting as it should and she might not make it through the night. Her twin, Tess, was pronounced "fine and healthy."

Subsequent tests revealed that Sarah also had brain damage, and the family was told that she would "never see, hear, walk or smell." Cognizant of the futility of heroic measures, Maureen and Jim decided to let nature take its course. Six weeks later, Sarah was brought home to join her well twin, Tess.

In time, Maureen went back to work and Jim, a graphic artist who worked at home, took care of Sarah and Tess. While antithetical to "what men are supposed to do," this nurturing role was one which Jim found "awesome." "I loved it," he said, "and would do it all over again."

Caring for Sarah was no easy task. She cried incessantly and vomited often. Irritable, she would stay up until 2 a.m., re-awakening four hours later. Hospice became involved, providing two hours of home health aide care and invaluable psycho-spiritual support, but Jim and Maureen remained the ultimate caregivers.

Fifteen weeks after the birth of the twins, Tess awoke and vomited at 3 a.m. A few hours later, she began sweating and was minimally able to be aroused from sleep. A call was made to 911 and within seven minutes an ambulance arrived and CPR was begun. Efforts to restart the infant's heart were futile and after one hour, all medical interventions ceased. Tess, the ostensibly healthy twin, was pronounced dead.

Overwhelmed with shock and sorrow, Jim and Maureen remained at the hospital and held their dead child for hours, until her tiny body began to feel cold. Prayers and a blessing were bestowed. A policeman drove Jim and Maureen home. "The wrong girl just died," thought Jim as he and his wife trudged upstairs to tell Hannah what had happened. That Tess died on Maureen's birthday rendered her demise even more poignant.

Maureen and Jim went through the motions of a private viewing and funeral for Tess. Incredulous friends and relatives came from near and far to offer supportive presence which was greatly appreciated by the grieving family. An autopsy later revealed that Tess had a rare disease, infantile arterial calcification. Apparently, both parents were carriers of the recessive gene.

Hannah, who was just six-years-old when Tess died, responded with sadness as well as childlike curiosity, asking questions such as "Will Tess turn into a skeleton right away?" No question was unacceptable to her parents who answered with patience and authenticity. For some time, the entire family received bereavement counseling at a grief and loss center known as "Peter's Place." Hannah also belonged to a support group at school for children who had siblings with disabilities.

After Tess died, Jim acknowledged feelings of resentment toward Sarah for about a week, but their routine was quickly resumed. A night nurse was hired to be with Sarah. After eight months she stopped vomiting and began to respond to external stimuli. She would smile and coo, batting at a mobile of seashells suspended above. Yet she was likened to a rag doll, unable to walk or even roll over.

Life enhancing interventions for Sarah were begun at home and, in time, she began to attend "a school" for children similarly affected. During this interim, a second healthy child, Liam, was born.

In the summer of 2006, the family took a vacation. During the trip, Maureen and Jim noticed some subtle changes in Sarah and were concerned, but upon returning home, she appeared normal. A lukewarm bath and backrub evoked a radiant smile. Jim checked on her at 4:30 a.m. that morning and heard her snoring. At 8 a.m., however, he found her with her mouth wide open. She was motionless . . . still as ice . . . and would not awaken. Jim tried mouth-to-mouth resuscitation to no avail, and once more, 911 was called. Maureen and Jim wept and held their dead child as Hannah cried out, "No... no... no!"

Sarah's memorial service was held in the family backyard, a scenic setting with trees like a cathedral.

Family members and invited guests wore their hair in the "pebbles" hairdo worn by Sarah. Hannah announced that the ritual would begin with the elephant sound which had always invariably evoked Sarah's laughter. Her favorite music was played and children participated. "The Invitation" by Oriah Mountain Dreamer was read; clearly it epitomized the transformation of the family. "We will never again be who we were" said Jim, adding that they now wear an invisible badge of honor. He added that, in times of suffering, "some people buy crutches; others grow wings." Maureen, Jim, Hannah and Liam are indeed winged spirits.

Sarah's mom and dad composed the following reflection which was read at Sarah's memorial service:

Who is Sarah?

So many conventional labels.
Sarah is our daughter.
She is sister to Hannah and Liam and she is Tess's twin.
Sarah is the one who was supposed to die three years ago.
From her first breath, Sarah carried enormous burdens. The burdens of survival — brain damage, heart failure, and profound disabilities. This robbed her of her potential, her peace, and of her pleasure. It would keep her reliant on the care of others for the rest of her life.
But beyond the labels, beyond the prognosis, and beyond the disease, there was your sunshine. The little girl who defied the odds and became such an important part of our extended family.
Sarah is the miracle that laughed and smiled and loved her family and friends for three years despite all predictions.
Sarah is the daughter that reveled in her mother's big belches and her father's ear-shattering sneezes.
Sarah is the sister that inspired patience, kindness, and unconditional love.
Sarah is the granddaughter that loved to be held and wear pretty dresses.
Sarah is Room 7's star pupil with the bright smile and the "pebbles" hair-do.
Sarah is the artist that created her own music and language with wind chimes, bells, kisses, and coos.
Sarah is the patient that baffled experts and forged new paths.
Sarah is the night owl who preferred to stay up for Letterman and sleep all morning.
Sarah is the friend who said "let down your guard for a moment and act silly — trumpet like an elephant just for me."
Sarah is the wisdom that taught us that life is neither fair nor unfair, but is short and should be pursued with zeal.
Sarah is the gift that showed us how to slow down and just be. Live in the moment. Just be home. Just be together. Just see the life teeming around us — even without the road trips, movies, restaurants, and action-packed schedules we sometimes bitterly missed.
Sarah is heartache of a future we will never know.

But today she is free — free of an earthly form that entrapped a soaring spirit; free to play with Tess as she was meant to; free to be a little girl.

Thanks to all of you who have made this journey with us. You are the glue that has held our family together during times of great joy and anguish. We could not have had Sarah in our lives and in our home everyday of her short life had it not been for your strength and support.

Take comfort in her freedom and in the fact that the heavens have grown so much richer with the newest Angel — Sarah.

Spiritual Exercise

Having reflected on the story of Sarah, as well as your own experience of loss, read the following poem by David Whyte:

The Well of Grief

Those who will not slip beneath
the still surface on the well of grief

Turning down through its black water
to the place we cannot breathe

will never know the source from which we drink,
the secret water, cold and clear,

nor find in the darkness glimmering
the small round coins
thrown by those who wished for something else.

David Whyte, from *Where Many Rivers Meet.* Copyright © 1990 by David Whyte. Many Rivers Press, Langley, WA.

JOTTINGS: _____

_____

_____

_____

What was it like for you to plumb the depths of the well of grief — or what has prevented you from doing so?

_____

_____

_____

_____

_____

_____

_____

_____

_____

_____

_____

_____

_____

_____

_____

_____

_____

To what extent have you, like Sarah's family, symbolically partaken of the cold, clear, source from which we drink — or discovered golden coins?

_____

_____

_____

_____

_____

_____

_____

_____

_____

_____

_____

_____

_____

_____

_____

_____

Epilogue: Lessons of Living Taught by the Dying

S poon River Anthology, by the American writer Edgar Lee Masters, is a collection of epitaphs in which deceased persons share the truth and wisdom of their lives, including both light and shadow. Similarly, some of the patients with whom I worked have written inscriptions for their own tombstones with the intention of sharing spiritual enlightenment born of their life experience. These are but a few excerpts from an informal work we lightly named *The Hudson River Anthology:*

A teacher, I doled out lesson after lesson, glibly preaching to my students, but it took me many years to learn to practice what I preached. *Teachers of others, are you failing to teach yourselves?*

My husband was a florist but the flowers of love in the garden of our lives soon withered and died, for we were too busy to tend to one another. *Take the time to nurture relationships.*

A waiter and a cook, I delayed until the eleventh hour to serve myself a huge helping of forgiveness. *Do not postpone the letting go of guilt, or self-recriminations, be they real or imagined.*

The closed door of my room was but a symbol of my stance toward life. Thus I lived in safety but rarely tasted, let alone savored, the bread of life. *Run the risk of opening your heart to love.*

As a funeral director, I created a cemetery of the heart by burying deep my human feelings. *Know that to harden your heart to sorrow is to render it impervious to joy as well.*

A physician, I could not cure myself and so was forced to drink the bitter potion of powerlessness. Mixed with trust, it proved to be a tonic of the spirit. *Power is made perfect in weakness.*

Though blind, I discovered sight in my fingertips and the light of joy in my heart. *To accept deprivation is to discover diviner gifts.*

Spiritual Exercise
Write some epitaphs for yourself, or for others.

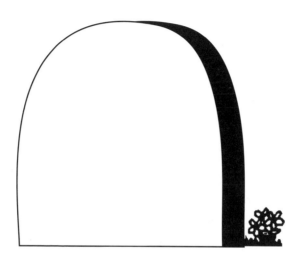

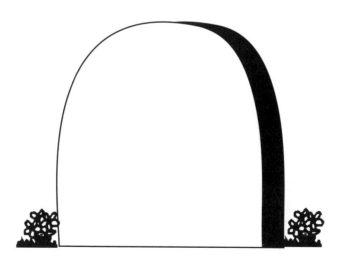

APPENDIX

Guided Meditation

The Colors of My Life

Find a quiet place where you will not be disturbed. Take a moment to be conscious of your breath, not seeking to change its pattern but simply becoming mindful of its ebb and flow . . . effortless . . . as mesmerizing as ocean waves. Become aware of any places of tension in your body and make a conscious effort to relax each part.

Now picture your heart as a large, empty canvas, devoid of any color, as we invite the Divine Artist, Memory, to create a painting of your life.

Envision yourself dipping the brush of your lived experience into the color yellow. Yellow is the color of daffodils . . . sunshine . . . feel the warmth of the sun on your face permeating every pore. Call to mind the sunshine moments of your life . . . times of lightheartedness . . . freedom . . . joy . . . enlightenment. Allow each image to appear, then fade as it is replaced by another . . . sunshine moments of your life and heart.

Now dip your brush into the color red, recreating the red moments of your life . . . Roses are red . . . red is the color of vibrancy . . . experiences of passion . . . love . . . anger. Once again, allow the images to come . . . see them . . . and let them go.

Envision the color black . . . black is the color of the sky at midnight, a color often associated with death . . . the dark night of the soul . . . depression . . . grief . . . take some time to visualize the black moments of your life . . . Look . . . listen . . . and learn what black has to teach you as you remember the sorrowful mysteries of your life.

Be mindful of the ebb and flow of ocean waves as we reflect on the color blue . . . azure skies . . . feeling blue . . . fresh blueberries . . . Taste, touch and feel the beauty of blue.

Now envision the color purple . . . Violets . . . and grapes . . . and some Easter eggs are purple. Bruises are often purple . . . Purple is also said to represent healing and harmony . . . the Divine Connection. Remember your own experiences of healing of body or spirit . . . times when you felt in harmony with creation . . . another person . . . God.

As I mention other colors, let your own associations be brought into the light of consciousness: green . . . springtime flowers pushing through the impossibility of winter . . . beginnings; white . . . the pristine purity of newly fallen snow . . . peace.

Brown . . . the color of the earth. Orange . . . bright and bold . . . pumpkins . . . autumn leaves . . . Pink . . . femininity . . . softness.

You have been painting an imaginary portrait of your life and heart. Take a moment to step back and look at it. Notice the array of colors . . . some perhaps more predominant than others. Take a long, loving look at this masterpiece painted with the brush of your life and colors of your experience. Take the time to admire . . . honor . . . and reverence this painting which is yet in process. You may wish to create an artistic representation of what this meditation was like for you.

Major Loss Inventory

Name loss (e.g. death, of loved one, loss of esteem, hope, faith, a pet, a job, a body part or physical ability, friendship, a loss inherent in a transition)	It was a time when . . . (express thoughts, feelings, circumstances of each loss)	Coping Mechanisms (What did I do to cope, confront or avoid the pain of loss?)	Degree of Resolution (Where am I on the continuum of healing?)

Guided Meditation

Hands

Assume a comfortable posture – eyes closed, hands resting in your lap, palms up. Spend a moment becoming aware of your breathing, not seeking to change its pattern, but simply being mindful of the breath as you gently inhale and exhale. Think of the air around you as an ocean of peace and serenity. As you breathe in, envision the air filling your entire being with tranquility; as you exhale, breathe out anxieties, worries and concerns. Breathe in peace, breathe out tension.

Become aware of the air at your fingertips, between your fingers, on the palm of your hands. Experience the fullness, strength and maturity of your hands. Think of your hands, think of the most unforgettable hands you have known – the hands of your father, your mother, your grandparents. Remember the oldest hands that have rested in your hands. Think of the hands of a new-born child – the incredible beauty, perfection, delicacy in the hands of a child. Once upon a time your hands were the same size.

Think of all that your hands have done since then. Almost all that you have learned has been through your hands – turning yourself over, crawling and creeping, walking and balancing yourself; learning to hold something for the first time; feeding yourself, washing and bathing, dressing yourself. At one time your greatest accomplishment was tying your own shoes.

Think of all the learning your hands have done and how many activities they have mastered, the things they have made. Remember the day you could write your own name.

Our hands are not just for ourselves, but for others. How often they were given to help another: Remember all the kinds of work they have done, the tiredness and aching they have known, the cold and the heat, the soreness and the bruises. Remember the tears they have wiped away, our own or another's, the blood they have bled, the healing they have experienced. How much hurt, anger and even violence they have expressed, and how much gentleness, tenderness and love they have given.

How often your hands have been folded in prayer; a sign of both powerlessness and power. Our fathers and mothers guided our hands in symbolic language — the sign of the cross, the handshake, the wave of a hand in "hello" or "good-bye".

There is a mystery which we discover in the hand of a woman or in the hand of a man that we love. There are the hands of a doctor, a nurse, an artist, a conductor, a priest, hands which you can never forget…

Think of all the hands that have left their imprint on you. Fingerprints and handprints are heartprints that can never be erased. The hand has its own memory. Think of all the places that people carry your handprints and all the people who bear your heartprint. They are indelible and will last forever…

Allow the faces of these people to pass before the screen of your mind, focusing on each one briefly, then letting it go.

Become mindful once more of your breath . Breathe in and out, in and out. Become aware of your hands, once again, resting in your lap…and when you feel ready, open your eyes and look at your hands, perhaps seeing them in a new light.

— Adaptation of Hands Meditation by Ed Farrell
from *Celtic Meditations*